The Women
of Montparnasse

The Women
of Montparnasse

Morrill Cody

With Hugh Ford

New York • Cornwall Books • London

306.0944
C671 w
1984

Cornwall Books
440 Forsgate Drive
Cranbury, NJ 08512

Cornwall Books
25 Sicilian Avenue
London WC1A 2QH, England

Cornwall Books
2133 Royal Windsor Drive
Unit 1
Mississauga, Ontario L5J 1K5, Canada

Library of Congress Cataloging in Publication Data

Cody, Morrill, 1901–
    The women of Montparnasse.

    Includes index.
    1. Montparnasse (Paris, France)—Intellectual life.
2. Paris (France)—Intellectual life.   3. Americans—
France—Paris.   4. British—France—Paris.
5. Women—France—Paris.   I. Ford, Hugh D., 1925–
II. Title.
DC752.M8C6   1983   306'.0944'361   81-71638
ISBN 0-8453-4747-0

Printed in the United States of America

Contents

Preface 7

Acknowledgments 17

Sylvia Beach 19

Josephine Baker 33

Hadley Hemingway 45

Nadia Boulanger 53

Zelda Fitzgerald 57

Peggy Guggenheim 66

Gertrude Stein 75

Nancy Cunard 89

Lady Duff Twysden 98

The Beautiful and the Loving 108

Mary Reynolds and Gala Eluard 123

Natalie Clifford Barney 132

Isadora Duncan 141

Margaret Anderson 149

Janet Flanner, Berenice Abbott, and Florence Gilliam 159

The Innkeepers 175

L'Envoi 187

Index 188

For Gabrielle

Preface

It is perhaps remarkable that the leaders and orga-
nizers of Montparnasse were largely women, from the
famed Kiki to the inspiring Sylvia Beach.

Morrill Cody, *Hemingway's Paris*

THE immense satisfaction of living in Paris in the twenties came from many
sources, which affected people in many different ways. Few of us who went
there remained untouched by these currents. To understand them and perhaps
experience something of their potency, one must look back to the early years
of this century, to the end of the Belle Epoque, that brief interlude of elegance
and charm and civilization that came to an abrupt close in 1914, at the start of
the First World War. As a child I passed the years from 1911 to 1914 at a
lycée near the gates of Paris, rebelling along with others against the excessive
discipline of the place and dreaming of what I would do when I next escaped
its forbidding confines. Usually the blessed release came on Sundays, when
for a few precious hours I would immerse myself in the warmth and calm of
Paris, or in the arboreal splendor of the Bois de Boulogne. The world turned
into a wonderful world indeed on Sundays. Everywhere I went I saw scenes
like those the impressionists had painted only a few years before. Though
barely an adolescent, I would roam the city alone, or with a school companion,
secure in the knowledge that wherever I strayed I would find friendliness and
kindness. Stability was the order of the day, and within that dependable
framework I discovered fun and laughter and a kind of love.

I did not see Paris again until 1921. By that time I had graduated from an
American college, and, at twenty, I wanted to return to the city that had given
me so many strong and fond memories. I was not disappointed. I spent the first
day revisiting all the places I had known and loved as a boy. I walked along
the Seine and through the Luxembourg Gardens, where children still sailed
their boats just as though nothing had happened in the years I had been gone.

The sight of those small handmade vessels majestically inching their way across a shallow pond assured me that somehow all was the same. No, nothing had changed. Paris, I naively thought, would again provide the constancy that had been the anchor of my youth.

But as I tried to reacquaint myself with the world I had once known, I noticed that the war had brought changes in those who had survived it and to the life of the country. The holocaust of Verdun still haunted the nation. The revolution in Russia had galvanized the hopes of many for profound political change in France and elsewhere in Europe. From the long quiescent working classes came cries for reforms never before voiced in France. Doubts about the conduct of the country's leaders during and after the war spiraled into loud and insistent demands for explanations and, more often, change, even at the cost of revolution.

Perhaps not a little of the unrest could also be traced to the extraordinary meetings that had occurred at every level between the French and the Americans who poured into the country in the final year of war. The Americans were not at all like the English, as the French thought they would be. They were much more friendly, much more kind, and much more boisterous, certainly less disciplined, and more fun. Sometimes they drank too much wine, and often they had too much money. *Beaux garçons* the French girls called them, and they found the Americans amazingly generous; and the French men, while understandably a little jealous, nevertheless admitted the Yanks could be brave and even fearless, but also foolhardy. Very quickly the Americans became the most popular foreigners in France. They could do no wrong, not really. If you were an American the twenties was a wonderful time and Paris a wonderful place in which to live, and this happy combination of time and place, I believe, created a very special atmosphere which lasted at least until the middle of the decade, and perhaps for a few fortunate ones well beyond.

When I speak of the Americans in Paris in the twenties—and the English who also came—I mean those who lived on the Left Bank and formed what might be called an Anglo-American colony there. They should not be confused with those dreary people—so we thought them to be at the time—who lived on the Right Bank and managed business affairs, who worked in the embassy, owned cars, lived in elegant apartments, and led depressingly unimportant lives. And when I speak of the Left Bank, I do not mean the entire region of the left side of the Seine, but only the Latin Quarter, which to some degree is still a students' and artists' quarter. We Left Bankers never crossed the Seine if we could avoid it, except of course to work on a job or to cash a check from home, an unpleasant but necessary duty. I might add that in those days no bank, French or foreign, even existed on the Left Bank.

Living in Paris in the early twenties was cheap. Though inflation and change would gradually push prices upward, for most of us the devaluation of the franc more than compensated for higher costs, that is, if you had dollars, or pounds sterling, or some other hard currency. Then one could manage to live in Paris for less than twenty-five dollars a month. Soon after my return I

A party in Rowley Smart's studio, Montparnasse, early 1920s *(Photo from the collection of Morrill Cody).*

got a job on the European edition of Colonel McCormick's *Chicago Tribune*. It paid only fifteen dollars a week, but it was enough for a small hotel room and food and an occasional drink at the Select or one of the other popular cafés in the neighborhood. Some of my friends with incomes of one hundred dollars a month lived very well, indeed, with their wife or partner. A young writer like Hemingway could get along—and did—on much less, however. And for the perennially impecunious artist a veritable warren of studios—over a hundred—existed in a single building in the rue Campaigne Première, near Boulevard Montparnasse. Of course, the amenities were decidedly minimal— no running water, no heat except what came from a potbellied stove in the middle of the room—but there was plenty of bright north light, plenty of good company nearby, and no worries. In those days for a few dollars one could always find such a studio.

I do not wish to overemphasize the thrift that often, and by necessity, engaged our lives in Paris. Not a few Americans as well as English had enough money to live a comfortable life in comfortable apartments, dine in restaurants that offered the *bonne cuisine française*, go to nightclubs in Montmartre, to the Opera and the Comédie Française, the music halls, and drink all they could hold at the Dingo Bar, where Jimmy the Barman held court, using the Dôme as a way station for an early aperitif. Many like myself, however, lacked private funds, regular allowances from parents, or savings accounts and small pensions from which to draw when necessary. We took jobs, perhaps on one of

Billy Lane, American artist, Paris, about 1925 *(Photo from the collection of Morrill Cody).*

Mary Coles, American painter, Paris, 1933 *(Photo from the collection of Morrill Cody).*

the five English-language newspapers then printed in Paris, or with the American or English news services. A few, very few, managed to sponge on the more affluent, but cadgers in Montparnasse usually had short careers.

Gertrude Stein is sometimes remembered for her pithy statements, several of which comment on the advantages of living in France. "It was not so much what France gave you," she once said, "it was what she did not take away." Gertrude, I believe, was speaking of freedom. In Paris, short of theft or injury of body to those around us, we felt free to do whatever we wanted. None of the moral restraints still so prevalent where we had come from endured there. Admittedly, the French sometimes complained that the restrictions on us were both fewer and lighter than those imposed on their own, who still had to think of family customs, religious scruples, respectability in the old-fashioned sense. But for us, few, if any, controls affecting the manner in which we chose to conduct our lives existed.

This freedom to live one's own life, to think one's own thoughts appealed not only to those who simply wanted to get away from it all, but also to those who felt that their creative ambitions had been stiffled and cramped by external forces at home. That the forces may often have been imagined is beside the point. The ones who developed their talents in Paris already possessed those talents before they arrived. There is little doubt that they would have developed them in almost any surroundings, but Paris allowed them to do it with a minimum of expense and in the stimulating company of fellow writers, artists, and musicians. Gertrude Stein, Djuna Barnes, Nancy Cunard, Ernest Hemingway, James Joyce, Robert McAlmon, and most of the others had been writing for some years before they settled in Paris. There they expanded without pressure.

As remarkable as it may seem, in those years in Montparnasse it was the women among us who shaped and directed and nourished the social and artistic and literary life of the young (under thirty) and vibrant Anglo-American art colony. Without them, the colony would have neither the historical richness nor the cultural significance that has made it for years such an absorbing subject. Resourceful, vital, resolute, and blessed with immense talent, the women left their mark on all they encountered. For the most part, by the time they came to Paris they had already detached themselves from their families, and very few ever allowed themselves to become encumbered with husbands or with children. Thus relieved of the customary time-consuming familial obligations and independent of men (if they wanted to be), they, like anybody else, were free to develop and exert their own ideas and theories of art, philosophy, and leadership, and to pursue as ardently as they wished whatever desires or ambitions had brought them to Paris. None as I recall ever suffered from timidity; all had migrated to Paris for a definite reason. Naturally, the serious ones came for study and for the chance to express themselves in the arts. Others, more circumspectly perhaps, sought love, or sex, or a reprieve from the social and moral restraints at home, such as Prohibition. And then there were still others, possibly a majority, who came expecting Paris to be a talisman that would help them discover who they were. More often than not the ageless search for identity produced at least one reward: it brought them into the company of others seeking the same end.

I have tried in this book to describe the women who for a variety of reasons came together in Montparnasse during the period between world wars. I have tried to show their astonishing diversity of character, their emotions, their sensibilities, and the intellectual drive that motivated them to seek and create and then inhabit their own special heaven on earth. Together they formed a ball of energy, a driving force of spirit and exhilaration, like a volcano pushing its way up from the lower world.

The women who possessed undeniable creative powers and achieved lasting fame—writers, artists, and musicians—were small in numbers, but, qualitatively, they formed a remarkably gifted group. One thinks immediately of Gertrude Stein because she publicized herself so ardently. If people refused to

A party in Rowley Smart's studio, Montparnasse, early 1920s *(Photo from the collection of Morrill Cody).*

read her books, or claimed they could not, they could hardly escape her public presence. Of those less inclined toward self-celebration and whose talents many would say were equal or even superior to Miss Stein's, several are notable: among the writers, the satirist Djuna Barnes, whom Janet Flanner would name "the most important writer" in Paris; Kay Boyle, whose fiction abounds with delicate responses to French life; Anaïs Nin, helpmate and supporter of Henry Miller and a writer of subtle power; the strikingly original poets Hilda Doolittle and Mina Loy; the English novelist Mary Butts, stormy and magnetic; and the peripatetic Janet Flanner (Genêt), whose fortnightly letters from Paris to the *New Yorker* achieved literary distinction. Their niche in modern writing is noteworthy and secure.

Daphne and Art Grand, Paris, mid-1920s *(Photo from the collection of Morrill Cody).*

With the possible exception of the artists Romaine Brooks, whose sojourns in Montparnasse usually consisted of lengthy stopovers with Natalie Clifford Barney in the rue Jacob, and Nina Hamnett, the English painter who shuttled between her studio (formerly Modigliani's) and Left Bank cafés, sketching and painting, few of the other women artists are remembered today. Berenice Abbott, however, perfected her photographic techniques to a degree achieved only by her mentor Eugène Atget; and the irrepressible Isadora Duncan fashioned an inimitable form of dance as spellbinding as the flamboyant life she led. In music, Nadia Boulanger taught and guided a group of talented young American composers that included Virgil Thomson, Aaron Copland, and Melville Smith; and Olga Rudge, a violinist from Cincinnati, who became Ezra Pound's lifetime companion, enjoyed a musical career of considerable prominence. Among the black entertainers who performed in Paris, a few

Lillian Fiske, wealthy American divorcée, Paris, 1927 *(Photo courtesy of Bill Widney).*

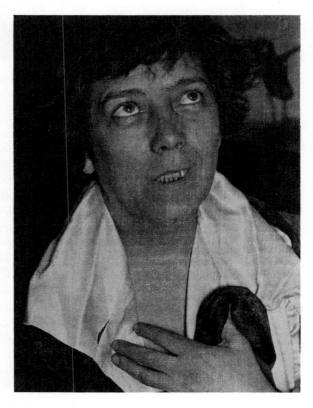

remained in the city and became immortal: Josephine Baker, the former
chorus girl who enraptured audiences at the Folies-Bergère for decades;
Bricktop, a redheaded singer and dancer whose clubs attracted royalty and
artists from every continent; and Mabel Mercer, Florence Mills, and Adelaide
Hall. All made Montparnasse their home.

**Peggy Stevens with her husband, Samuel Putnam, author and editor of *The New
Review*, Paris, 1927 *(Photo courtesy of Bill Widney)*.**

Some women gained reputations as literary handmaidens. Sylvia Beach, for
example, although she had no literary self-expression, made a contribution to
literature far more important, in my opinion, than that of Gertrude Stein. The
same might be said of her friend Adrienne Monnier, who guided Sylvia into
the intricacies of bookselling and publishing and whose own publications and
literary soirées served to unite French and English-speaking writers in Paris.
Outstanding among the industrious editors and publishers were Margaret Anderson and Jane Heap, the colorful directors of the *Little Review*; Nancy
Cunard, who founded her own press to print whatever seemed "modern";
Maria Jolas, who with her husband, Eugene, directed the idiosyncratic review
transition; Ethel Moorhead, a strong-minded Scot and ex-suffragette who
poured a fortune into another review, *This Quarter*; and Barbara Harrison,
who supported the most sumptuous of the little presses in Paris. Three of these
women—Margaret Anderson, Nancy Cunard, and Maria Jolas—developed
into important literary artists on their own.

Of course many were in Paris for reasons less memorable or meaningful.
They came there to play, to entertain and be entertained, to watch and be
watched, and some of them almost made an art of it, such as the magnetic
real-life Lady Brett Ashley in Hemingway's novel *The Sun Also Rises*, Lady
Duff Twysden; and Zelda Fitzgerald; and the inspiring model Kiki; and Flossie Martin, a New York chorus girl whose personality, good looks, infectious

Revelers at the Bal Negre, annual costume ball attended by many Americans, Moulin de la Galette, Montmartre, mid-1920s *(Photo from the collection of Morrill Cody).*

gaiety, and warm heart captivated multitudes of admirers. They could be more fun on a Saturday night in Montmartre than, say, Sylvia Beach, although it was hard sometimes to remember on Sunday morning just why you had thought it such a glorious evening.

And then there were the women who played a less dramatic role, yet brought needed consolation and advice and, at times, support to the men and women who floundered along because of some maladjustment of money or love. Jopie Wilson, the sympathetic patronne of the Dingo Bar, and Rosalie, who fed the artists and writers from her little restaurant on the rue Campaigne Première, and Madame Pons in her student hotel on the rue Bernard Palissy, and also Madame Camille, who held sway over the Trois et As Bar on the rue Tournon—all selflessly provided others with the human underpinnings they needed. Hadley Hemingway was a comforting person, and so were Kitty Cannell, a quiet, reserved, friendly intellectual girl from Boston, and Jo Bennett, who kept that patriarch of the expatriates, Harold Stearns, from falling apart completely.

Providing comfort in more material ways were such women as Caresse Crosby, wife of the Morgan heir Harry Crosby; Natalie Clifford Barney, a rich Ohioan who founded a colony of women artists in honor of Sappho; the eccentric Princess, Eugène Murat; and the art collector Peggy Guggenheim, who inspired and assisted several major artists of the century.

Alexander Calder at exhibit "American Writers in Paris and Their Friends," Paris, 1959 *(Photo from the collection of Morrill Cody).*

I have always thought that the Americans and English in the quarter—women and men—could be placed into one of three groups: first, those serious people, principally writers and artists, who worked all day and played in the early evening, and perhaps also on weekends; second, those who worked a little, played rather hard, and made love with serious intent; and then the others, who always said they worked at something but never really applied themselves. They played all night and slept it off all day. The first group was by far the largest, but it was the last group that made the most noise and earned for Montparnasse the intriguing but misleading reputation as a place where people dissipated themselves and frittered away their time and talent.

A party in Rowley Smart's studio, Montparnasse, early 1920s *(Photo from the collection of Morrill Cody).*

With all their freedom, Left Bankers did not descend into debauchery, or decline into any special overindulgence, as some have contended in books about Paris in the twenties. Yes, we used our freedoms to the fullest, but what we did was done openly, without constraint by custom or moralistic authorities. And as for the "Lost Generation" tag, we were no more lost than those who remained at home. We were simply better off in mind and spirit.

Acknowledgments

FOR valuable assistance in gathering materials, including photographs, for this book, the authors wish to thank Sue Pattou, Therese Ford, Olivia Harlan, the late Sara Ullman, Bill Widney, Virgil Thomson, Allen Tanner, Mark Turbyfill, Jacques Baron, Julie Groff, Tom and Doloris Wood, Charles E. Greene, Professor Carlos Baker, Professor Kenneth Wheeler, Professor Virginia Lussier, George Wickes, Holly Fullam, and Juliet Man Ray.

Sylvia Beach

THE most remarkable characteristic of Montparnasse in the twenties was, in my opinion, the way French, American, English, and Irish writers were drawn together to talk and to read each other's works. From this penetrating experience they undoubtedly learned more than they would have absorbed from any other comparable source. Largely responsible for this amalgam of ideas were two gifted women, Sylvia Beach and Adrienne Monnier, who have never been given full credit for their achievement.

When I returned to Paris in 1923, my wife, Frances, and I carried three letters of introduction given us by her friend, English Walling, a New York writer who had visited Paris the previous year. The letters were addressed to Ernest Hemingway, "a young newspaperman who may be fun," William Bird, another journalist of somewhat longer standing, and Sylvia Beach, "who runs a little shop on the Left Bank named Shakespeare and Company." All three became lifelong friends, but I headed first for Sylvia Beach, as I had an assignment from *Publishers Weekly* to do a piece about her remarkable shop.

She received me cordially, as she received everyone, smiling at me and inviting me to sit down. Sylvia had the brightest and sharpest blue eyes I have ever seen, unforgettable, intelligent, but also most kindly. I gave her my letter and asked if she would give me information on which to base an article about Shakespeare and Company, her little shop at 12 rue de l'Odeon.

"Of course I will," she replied, and we went to work at once. She later told me that this was the first article about her bookshop to appear on either side of the Atlantic.

Sylvia was the daughter of a Presbyterian minister in Princeton, New Jersey, who had at an earlier time been the director of an American artists' center in Paris, and Sylvia had thus spent five years in Paris, beginning at the age of fourteen. She had fallen in love with Paris and with France, as so many

19

**Sylvia Beach (right) with her sister, Holly, Shakespeare and Company, 8 rue Dupuy-
tren, Paris, 1919** *(Photo from the papers of Sylvia Beach, Princeton University
Library).*

English and Americans have done, and she was fortunate in knowing it during
the Belle Epoque. Even after she went to Princeton with her father, she
continued to visit Paris regularly for vacations and study. Her interest was
always in books, and she dreamed one day of having a bookshop in New York
where she might sell the works of French writers of the then modern school.
But, alas, she did not have the financial backing for such a project, but
perhaps, she thought, something would one day turn up to facilitate her
ambition. It did, but not in quite the way she had anticipated.

In 1916 Sylvia was living in one of those delightful apartments of the Palais
Royal with her sister, Cyprian. One day she read in a French literary journal
an item about a bookshop on the Left Bank called La Maison des Amis des
Livres, the house of the friends of books. Who was a greater friend of books
than Sylvia? She rushed off to explore this shop which had extended a welcom-
ing hand through its name. There she met the owner, Adrienne Monnier, a
kindred soul if ever there was one. Their acquaintance ripened into a deep
friendship and a determination that Sylvia, too, must have her bookshop. At
first, they thought it should be a branch of La Maison des Amis des Livres in
New York, but that idea was abandoned when they realized the high costs

Sylvia Beach in her bookshop, 12 rue de l'Odeon, Paris, 1921 *(Photo from the papers of Sylvia Beach, Princeton University Library).*

involved. La Maison des Amis des Livres ran on a shoestring and could not support a branch anywhere. Adrienne Monnier had started her little shop in the hope of attracting the writers and readers of the new trends in French literature. She had succeeded. They were attracted first by the warm character of this little woman with her gray blue eyes, fair hair and skin, her unusual clothes, which seemed to be half nun and half peasant, and by her mind, quick and alert. To her shop came André Gide, Valéry Larbaud, Jules Romains, Paul Valéry, Paul Claudel, and many other literary giants of the time. They came to browse, to talk, and on occasion to recite their works. The Maison was more of a club and a lending library than a bookshop. Sylvia saw at once that Adrienne had already created the kind of atmosphere that she dreamed of having. The idea of a French bookshop in New York was abandoned and the concept of an Anglo-American literary gathering place in Paris was born.

In the initial phases, Adrienne was an asset of immense value. She knew the hows and whys of dealing with landlords, carpenters, plumbers, and government offices. It was Adrienne who found the very small shop for rent in the nearby rue Dupuytren, not far from Adrienne's shop. A couple of years later Sylvia was able to move to a better shop directly across the street from the Maison des Amis des Livres. Here Shakespeare and Company flourished spiritually, if not materially. Here came Ernest Hemingway, James Joyce, Gertrude Stein, F. Scott Fitzgerald, Robert McAlmon, Janet Flanner, Ford Madox Ford, Kay Boyle, and many, many more. This, too, became a club and a lending library rather than a bookshop because the prices of English and American books were so high when translated into French francs. They came to read and to browse and to borrow and occasionally to buy. The little shop barely survived, financially, but it was a joyous and inspiring place to gather. Soon, too, the French writers around the Maison and the Anglo-Americans and Shakespeare and Company began, slowly, to merge, to know each other's works, and to form lasting friendships. "Sylvia Beach carried pollen like a bee," André Chamson said. "She cross-fertilized these writers. She did more to link England, the United States, Ireland, and France than four great ambassadors combined." Sylvia had opened her bookshop at exactly the right time, November 19, 1919. The war was over and the influx of Americans was just beginning. And so she was in Paris at the start of this remarkably creative period in literature.

Most of the meager financial support for Shakespeare and Company came from the fees paid by subscribers for the right to borrow a book or two for a period of two weeks. The world for subscriber in French is *abonné*. Holly, Sylvia's other sister, immediately began calling subscribers the "bunnies," and bunnies they remained for everyone thereafter. It is interesting to note that the first three bunnies were all French, André Gide being one of them. Other early bunnies were Gertrude Stein and Alice B. Toklas. And as bunnies always do, they multiplied quickly until the little shop was as crowded as the Maison across the street.

The relationship between Sylvia and Gertrude Stein was an off and on affair. At first, they seemed to like each other, but when Sylvia began the publication of James Joyce's *Ulysses*, Gertrude and Alice canceled their subscriptions and severed relations. Gertrude could not imagine that anyone would choose to publish Joyce instead of Stein! Sylvia's comment about Gertrude and Alice in her autobiography is astute: "Alice had a great deal more finesse than Gertrude. And she was grown up; Gertrude was a child, something of an infant prodigy." But later Sylvia and Gertrude made up their differences by agreeing never to mention Joyce. In that period Sylvia would bring many visitors to the studio in the rue de Fleurus to meet "La Stein." Everybody, it seemed, wanted to meet Gertrude, and most of them did because she liked such attention. The way to meet Gertrude was to arrange matters with Sylvia Beach. Meeting Gertrude was like taking a special tour of Paris by night.

Sylvia first met James Joyce at a party, and they were greatly taken with each other. She had, of course, read all of his works that had been printed and also the parts of *Ulysses* which had appeared in Margaret Anderson's *Little Review*. She was deeply impressed with his literary talent. The day after the party Joyce came around to see her and poured out to her willing ear all his problems. In New York, protectors of the public morals had seized copies of the *Little Review*, and the entire work was now prohibited in the United States. In England, Harriet Weaver, who had intended to publish *Ulysses* as soon as Joyce finished it, decided that it would encounter similar difficulties there and postponed publication temporarily. Meanwhile, Joyce had a family of four to house and feed, and he was still writing the last part of *Ulysses*. In Trieste, where he had lived before coming to Paris, he had earned a living by teaching English, but now his need to finish his book was so strong that he could not focus his attention on any other activity. Sylvia was sympathetic, but she had no money to lend him. Nevertheless the idea of publishing his great work was intriguing. She thrust it away at first as impossible of fulfillment, but slowly she became possessed by it.

Joyce was a thin man of medium height. His manner and carriage did not indicate his inner strength. His handshake was limp, his eyes watery, his manner formal and somewhat distant. He expected to be called "Mr. Joyce," and not even Sylvia got around to addressing him otherwise, although he, of course, called her "Sylvia."

When Sylvia decided to publish *Ulysses*, she made careful preparations to be sure that the venture did not put her into bankruptcy. She found a printer in Dijon who was prepared to wait for payment for his work until the book was actually on sale and whose fees in any case were unusually small. The book was big, 877 pages, and Joyce made so many corrections and additions on the galley proofs that he increased the size of the book considerably. But Sylvia plodded on with all these trials and tribulations, lending Joyce money in small quantities, denying herself everything in order to get the book in print. Joyce was grateful, but his ego did not really permit him to understand the sacrifices

Sylvia Beach in conference with James Joyce, Shakespeare and Company, 1921 or 1922 *(Photo from the papers of Sylvia Beach, Princeton University Library).*

Sylvia was making for him. The book was finally published on Joyce's birth-day, February 2, 1922. It was an event of international literary importance that made Sylvia, as well as Joyce, famous around the world.

The following year, when I first met Sylvia, I obtained, through her good offices, an exclusive interview with Joyce. It has often been said that Joyce *never* gave an interview, but mine was the exception that proved the rule. It was published in the *Baltimore Sun,* a paper for which I did occasional features.

Joyce's basic ingratitude toward Sylvia showed itself more markedly in later years. When publication of *Ulysses* was finally permitted in both Britain and the United States, Joyce went off on his own to make contracts with commer-cial publishers, leaving Sylvia completely out of the negotiations and keeping all the benefits for himself, even though she had undeniable rights as its first publisher. But she was not going to fight with the man whose work she so admired. Joyce's greatest personal pleasure was spending money, often lav-ishly, and never on himself. He liked to give presents, especially to his wife, Nora, and to entertain in good restaurants where he bought fine wines and succulent dishes. He himself drank a very ordinary white wine and ate almost nothing. Joyce was devoted to his wife and children, Lucia and Giorgio. But the devotion of James Joyce and Nora had no literary flavor. She boasted that she had no interest in his writings and would never bother to read *Ulysses*. She didn't quite say that they were above her; she just implied it.

The most remarkable characteristic of Nora Joyce was her silence. In the presence of her husband she would sit demurely, looking interested, smiling a little now and then. But it is true that no one else said very much when James Joyce was around either, except to the Master himself. This was just as well, for Joyce was an interesting man to listen to, but a difficult person with whom to hold any kind of discussion.

When her husband was not around, Nora would chat in hospitable fashion with friends, especially women, about her household affairs or other mundane matters. People liked Nora, and she was welcome at any of the parties when she accompanied Joyce. I do not think she ever went alone.

After the publication of *Ulysses*, Sylvia was besieged with offers of erotic manuscripts to publish, which she rejected immediately. She had not published *Ulysses* because of its erotic character, and she had no intention of becoming a specialist in that field. Furthermore, she had her hands full handling one author and she did not want to take on another. It was amusing, however, to see the persons who flocked to her shop, manuscripts in hand. Among them was Frank Harris with the story of *My Life and Loves*. He could not understand why she rejected it without even reading it. Tallulah Bankhead was another who wished to be taken by Shakespeare and Company for the publication of her memoirs, in which she would tell all her secrets, and D. H. Lawrence was most persistent in his efforts to get Sylvia to publish *Lady Chatterley's Lover*. Still another was the mysterious and somewhat frightening Aleister Crowley with his *Diary of a Drug Fiend*. On the lighter side was the maître d'hôtel of Maxim's, who said he was ready to tell all about the high and mighty who had dined in his restaurant.

But her fame in the world of books did not lessen Sylvia's interest in writers, and in the course of the next ten years she came to know most of those who flourished in that period. There was a particular attachment between Ernest Hemingway and his wife Hadley and both Sylvia and Adrienne Monnier. They were helpful to him in the early years, for it was through Sylvia that he found Jonathan Cape, who became his British publisher, and it was Adrienne who translated the first of his stories to appear in French in her little magazine, *Le Navire d'Argent*.

Another close friend was Bryher, the wife of Robert McAlmon and the daughter of Sir John Ellerman, the shipping tycoon. Sir John and his wife wanted their daughter to enjoy all the benefits of their money and social position, but Anne Winifred would have none of it. To escape her parental tutelage she married McAlmon soon after she met him, which meant that he never lacked for money while she was free to do as she pleased. She assumed the name Bryher because it was that of one of the Scilly Islands where she had vacationed as a child. While her husband led an extravagant and bohemian life in Paris, Bryher sought seclusion in the country to write poetry. On rare

Sylvia Beach in front of her bookshop with her "best customer," Ernest Hemingway, mid-1920s *(Photo from the papers of Sylvia Beach, Princeton University Library).*

F. Scott Fitzgerald and Adrienne Monnier sitting at the entrance of Shakespeare and Company, 1928 *(Photo from the papers of Sylvia Beach, Princeton University Library).*

Sylvia Beach, Paris, 1959

occasions she visited her husband in Paris and always spent considerable time with Sylvia and Adrienne. She also used her money to help needy writers, particularly in later years when she aided victims of Nazi persecution to escape to the United States.

The number of Sylvia's friends is too long to give here, but it included such diverse personages as Edouard Herriot, the prime minister of France, and young writers such as André Chamson, André Maurois, Archibald MacLeish, Thornton Wilder, and Sherwood Anderson. To have so many friends meant that she gave part of her time to them, while also running a bookshop, caring for Joyce's eye troubles, seeing that he had sufficient money to make him happy, and bringing out edition after edition of *Ulysses*.

In the middle thirties, with the departure for home of most of her American bunnies and the falling off of the tourist stream, Sylvia's financial troubles became more and more acute. When she was on the verge of giving up her labors, the French writers gathered around to help her by subscribing money and by holding readings of their works at Shakespeare and Company for which admission was charged. This kept her going, but it was hard. And by this time she was feeling tired and somewhat played out. But she kept on just the same. When the war came she was urged to return to America, but she refused and even when her own country became involved she stayed on at 12 rue de l'Odeon.

Then one day a high-ranking Nazi officer came into the shop and in perfect English demanded to purchase a copy of Joyce's *Finnegans Wake*, which he had seen displayed in the window. Sylvia said she was sorry but it was not for sale since it was the only copy she had and was inscribed to her by the author. The officer became very insistent, and when he left, empty-handed, he said he would be back to confiscate that and other books. Sylvia was frightened; her only source of funds was the books and manuscripts that she had collected and could sell if need be. That afternoon and evening she and the concierge and a couple of friends moved all the books, papers, pictures, and furniture to an empty apartment on the third floor. She even painted out the sign over the door and had a carpenter take down all the built-in bookshelves. Shakespeare and Company had disappeared completely, except of course that Sylvia still lived on the second floor. Whether the officer really came back she never knew. But it was the end of the bookshop, which was erased as though it had never existed.

Sylvia stayed on in France, first for six months in an internment camp and, later, when a conditional residence permit was granted to her, in a small room in a student hostel attached to the University of Paris. In any case, it was too late to leave the country. She visited the empty shop and her apartment above it almost daily, but she never saw the Nazi officer again, and her books and papers were never molested. Her only chore was to report to the police once a week.

Then, in 1944, when the Germans were starting to leave Paris, she returned to her apartment in the rue de l'Odeon, even though sniper shooting was still going on along the street and from the rooftops. She saw no Allied soldiers, however, until one morning when Ernest Hemingway suddenly appeared at her door to say that he had come to "liberate" her. After that happy reunion he went on across the river to liberate the bar of the Ritz Hotel.

But Sylvia did not reopen her shop. She was tired and somewhat discouraged. Also, for the moment at least, she had no ready customers, and it would be some time before the American literary people would return to Paris, if indeed they ever did. She realized that the era in which Shakespeare and Company had a role to play was over. But she stayed on in Paris, writing her

Arthur Moss, Sylvia Beach, Thornton Wilder, Morrill Cody, Man Ray, and Alice B. Toklas on a café terrace, recreated for the exhibit "American Writers in Paris," Paris, 1959 *(Photo from the collection of Morrill Cody)*.

Arthur Moss, James Jones, Sylvia Beach, Thornton Wilder, and Alice B. Toklas, chatting at "American Writers in Paris" exhibit, Paris, 1959 *(Photo from the collection of Morrill Cody)*.

memoirs in a lovely book called simply *Shakespeare and Company*, published in 1959.

It was during this period that I was in charge of the cultural relations section of the American embassy in Paris, and it occurred to me that the time was ripe to have a retrospective exhibit of the great Anglo-Irish, French-American literary flowering which had existed in the twenties in Paris, and I naturally turned to Sylvia Beach for assistance. She welcomed the idea with immense enthusiasm. Many others besides Sylvia contributed their treasures, such as William Bird and his daughter France, Margaret Anderson, Mrs. J. S. Bradley, the Dudley sisters, Florence Gilliam, Maria Jolas, Man Ray, and Alice B. Toklas. Under the guiding hand of the embassy's gifted exhibits officer, Darthea Speyer and her staff, we collected more than two thousand first editions, manuscripts, photographs, drawings, and other mementos of the twenties. We reconstructed a little café with the iron tables and chairs of the period, and somewhere the staff found a player piano which, from a paper roll, belched forth the pounding music of the *Ballet Mécanique*. I invited all the literary people of the twenties I could find. Many came but, alas, many had to refuse for health reasons, such as Margaret Anderson, T. S. Eliot, Ernest

Sylvia Beach and Arthur Moss, "American Writers in Paris" exhibit, Paris, 1959
(Photo from the collection of Morrill Cody).

Sylvia Beach (center) with friends (left to right) Florence Gilliam, Martin Engleman, Arthur Moss, SB, Mme. Balthrusaites, and two unidentified men. "American Writers in Paris" exhibit, Paris, 1959. Portrait of Sylvia Beach on wall was painted by Paul-Emile Bécat *(Photo from the collection of Morrill Cody).*

Hemingway, and Bill Bird, among others. But Alice B. Toklas was there under the guiding hand of Thornton Wilder, and Maria Jolas, Florence Gilliam, and André Chamson all came. The list is, happily, a long one. The occasion was momentous. French and British and American authorities were also there. After a two-month showing in Paris, to great crowds daily, the exhibit was taken to London for another two-month run. The French government also wanted to take it to the United States under their auspices, but they did not immediately make up their minds, and Sylvia sold all the most important pieces to various American universities, and thus they were suddenly unavailable. In 1977, the new Pompidou Museum made an even larger exhibit on the same subject, but without many of the first editions which had marked the one in the rue du Dragon.

In 1962 I was living in Washington, but came on a visit to Paris in September of that year, and of course I saw Sylvia. She was just the same as ever, lively, enthusiastic, her blue eyes sparkling as before. On the evening of October 4 we both attended a party at the home of Darthea Speyer. I again marveled at the vitality and energy of Sylvia Beach. When the party was over,

Sylvia Beach and Morrill Cody, "American Writers in Paris" exhibit, Paris, 1959
(Photo from the collection of Morrill Cody).

I drove her back to her little apartment in the rue de l'Odeon. Not that night, but the next, she died in her sleep, seemingly without suffering.

She had left instructions that on her death she was to be cremated and buried in Père Lachaise cemetery. And so two days later, some forty or fifty of us went to the little chapel of the Colombarium in Père Lachaise. After we had waited for at least an hour, an attendant brought forth a small box covered with a green velvet cloth. He walked among us. Not a word was said. And then he disappeared through a door to the main building. It was an unworthy end to such a great person. Afterwards, her friend and admirer Janet Flanner wrote that Sylvia "always gave more than she received." No epitaph could contain a greater truth.

Josephine Baker

WHEN Josephine Baker arrived in Montparnasse in 1925 she was barely eighteen years old, almost totally uneducated, and not really pretty. Even her singing voice was almost nonexistent. But she was gay, very bright, and quick to learn from everybody. She had magic in her feet, which seemed to throw off electric sparks when she danced, and a bewitching, enticingly warm smile. She was a born comic who could make people laugh by distorting her face, blowing up her cheeks, crossing her eyes. Naturally, in 1925, she was not yet a star. But she was a member of Catherine Dudley's chorus line in "La Revue Nègre," the first black stage company ever brought to Europe from the United States. The show starred Florence Mills and Sidney Bechet, the jazz soprano saxophonist. Josephine, however, had a little more than a place in the chorus. She did a small dance routine.

Catherine Dudley was anxious to keep the members of her company together as much as possible, and so she rented an entire hotel for them, a small one, on the rue Campagne Première, just off the Boulevard Montparnasse. They sprawled all over the quarter, and we were delighted to see them.

Josephine, who had had some reservations about traveling to a foreign country, was enchanted with France from the first moment she saw the port of Cherbourg, and she was overwhelmed to find that the French treated black people just the way they treated whites or anyone else. She had been brought up in the black slums of Saint Louis, where she was born in 1906, in living conditions not fit for animals, much less for human beings. Although her own family was loving and did their best to provide for her, she had bitter memories of the treatment she had received at the hands of some whites and also at the hands of some overbearing black bullies. Even on the *Berangeria*, the American ship the troupe had taken for the crossing from New York, she and her companions had been sequestered in a small "reservation" below decks so that they could not possibly mix with the white passengers. Yet, behold! When they entered the dining car of the French train taking them to Paris, they were seated with white people and served by white waiters! Josephine could hardly believe her eyes. She knew she was going to love France. And as it turned out France adored her. From that first day in the country she saw that racism need not exist in the world and that she, Josephine Baker, was going to show the world that people with different colored skins could live happily together. It became her lifelong crusade.

When "La Revue Nègre" opened at the most prestigious music hall in Paris, the Théâtre des Champs-Elysées, at the end of September, Josephine became an instant success of overwhelming dimensions. Not only was the dancing spectacular, the music maddening, but the sets and costumes designed by Fernand Leger were superb. Of the entertainer's electrifying opening night Janet Flanner wrote:

> She made her entry entirely nude except for a pink flamingo feather between her limbs; she was being carried upside down and doing the split on the shoulder of a black giant. Midstage he paused, and with his long fingers holding her basketwise around the waist, swung her in a slow cartwheel to the stage floor, where she stood, like his magnificent descarded burden, in an instant of complete silence. She was an unforgettable female ebony statue. A scream of salutation spread through the theatre.

Josephine Baker, in Berlin, 1926 *(Photo from the Collection of American Literature Beinecke Rare Book and Manuscript Library, Yale University)*.

Whatever happened next was unimportant. The two specific elements had been established and were unforgettable—her magnificent dark body, a new model that to the French proved for the first time that black was beautiful, and the acute response of the white masculine public in the capital of hedonism of all Europe—Paris.*

And as the production was changed and improved from week to week, almost day to day, Josephine began to emerge as the real star of the performance. She was given solo roles and eventually she left the chorus line, forever as it turned out. Much of her success and growing importance to the performance as a whole was due to excellent French directors who recognized her amazing talents. When the Paris run ended, the troupe went on a European tour, and everywhere enthusiastic audiences lavished applause on Josephine. But still she was not the star. Then one day the director of the Folies-Bergère in Paris

*Janet Flanner. *Paris Was Yesterday*. (New York: Viking Press, 1972), pp. xx–xxi.

Josephine Baker, in Berlin, 1926 *(Photo from the Collection of American Literature Beinecke Rare Book and Manuscript Library, Yale University)*.

handed her a contract she could not refuse. It made her the star of a new company to be called "La Folie du Jour." Although she had already reached the pinnacle of music hall fame, this was Josephine's first role as *the* star. There, wearing her skirt of bananas, she introduced the Charleston to the French, who soon began calling her "La Ba-kair" and then simply "Jasephine." The show was a tremendous success, the first of many such successes that extended over many years in Paris and on tour to all corners of the earth.

I had seen Josephine in Montparnasse and on the stage, but it was not until fall of 1926 that I saw her at close range. The occasion was the gala ball of the Anglo-American Press Association, a group of professional newspapermen who annually gathered at the Claridge Hotel for an evening of eating, drinking, and entertainment, strictly for men only. This year the *pièce de resistance* was Josephine Baker, and about ten members of the "Folie du Jour" company.

Josephine Baker, in white tie and tails, Paris, late 1920s *(Photo from the Dance Collection, The New York Public Library at Lincoln Center, Astor, Lenox and Tilden Foundations).*

The tables of the banquet hall were arranged in a U-shape and the guests of honor, sitting at the bottom of the U, included the British ambassador, Sir Eric Drummond (if I remember correctly); the American ambassador, the much admired Myron T. Herrick; and the Paris préfet of police. The rest of us sat on either side of the U while the performers occupied the center space. Josephine and her companions appeared for the finale, dancing their exotic rhythms and then shedding their clothes piece by piece until they were almost naked. Suddenly, and with the agility of a leopard, Josephine jumped clear across the head table and landed in the lap of Sir Eric, who sputtered in a sort of protest. Immediately the British correspondents collectively rose to their feet, remarking, "I say! This is going too far. His Majesty's ambassador! Someone stop her!" Ambassador Herrick, I am happy to report, was the first man to take in the situation. Bending over, he quickly took Josephine in his arms, held her high above his head, kissed her on both cheeks, and gently set her down on her feet. Smiling she ran off quickly to her dressing room. We all shouted and cheered our approval, including the British journalists, who had been so indignant only a few minutes before. It was a night no one present ever forgot, I feel sure.

Of course an international stage sensation as successful as Josephine was bound to collect many suitors, not a few of them rich men who wanted nothing less than to marry her. Patou started giving her clothes, and the young son of a French auto family gave her a car a block long. Bewildered by all the attention, she would often turn for advice to another black entertainer, Bricktop, who herself had arrived in Paris only the year before Josephine. She became her confidante and would talk to Josephine "like a big sister." She advised Josephine to avoid entanglements that might interfere with her career. Josephine agreed and kept busy improving herself, training her voice, her diction, and her stage presence. Besides, she also wanted to enjoy the fame and excitement that came with her popularity. Nevertheless one of her suitors, whom she had met through still another admirer named Zito, a well-known caricaturist, particularly interested her. He was attractive. He also wanted to become her manager. His name was Count Abatino, but in Paris café society everyone called him by his nickname, Count Pepito. Though he was reputedly a millionaire industrialist, there were some like Bricktop who remembered that Pepito was also called "Count of No Account, because he didn't even have the price of a drink at the bar in Zelli's, where Zito worked—and because he was no account." Bricktop urged Josephine to play for bigger stakes than Pepito, since any number of Frenchmen were hers for the taking. But Josephine liked Pepito; she liked him so well she told him what Bricktop had said. After that the two women had to see each other when Pepito was away. Pepito, according to Bricktop, "stopped Josephine from running around, took her away from everybody . . . started her studying French and Italian (Pepito was Italian), taught her about painting and music—really sending her to school like a child. He got her a dancing master and a dramatic

Josephine Baker, at work, wearing a modified version of her famous banana costume, 1936 (Photo from the Dance Collection, The New York Public Library at Lincoln Center, Astor, Lenox and Tilden Foundations).

coach." He arranged her tours in Europe and South America and gave her personal guidance.

For ten years he devoted himself to Josephine. Of course he, too, wanted to marry her, and for awhile she stubbornly resisted his proposals. She said she was not ready for marriage. But then in June 1927, on her twenty-first birth-

Josephine Baker, resplendent in a Siamese costume she wore as a star of the Folies-Bergère, 1930s *(Photo from the Dance Collection, The New York Public Library at Lincoln Center, Astor, Lenox, and Tilden Foundations).*

day, she did marry Pepito, secretly. Two weeks later and after many denials Josephine hosted a party at her cabaret in the rue Fontaine and explained, when asked why they had kept their marriage a secret, that since she was only twenty-one and had never "got married before," she just "didn't know what to do." For the entertainment of the press and her friends, she slipped on her wedding ring for the first time in public and helped Pepito distribute the confetti.

It was Pepito who persuaded her to open her cabaret in Paris and similar clubs in other cities during her tours; they were always called Chez Josephine. The rich and the famous flocked to her cabaret and waited for her to appear after her evening appearance at the Folies-Bergère. Among her closest friends in this period were Jean Cocteau and Colette. Both found her amusing and exotic. Josephine shared with Colette a particular love of animals—cats, dogs, monkeys, and even snakes. Josephine sometimes wore a live snake around her neck when she arrived at a party or at her nightclub, much to the horror of some people.

Of course Josephine had long since moved from the little hotel in Montparnasse. Now she stayed in some of the big luxury establishments on the Right Bank. But even here American racism followed her across the Atlantic. Some hotel managers, reluctantly to be sure, indicated that they could not keep her "because their American clients objected." The plight of the hotel managers was understandable, so she took an apartment and that problem was solved, but it left a little bitterness with Josephine.

With great fame she also experienced that separation that perhaps inevitably divides the star from the people who were once very close companions and even friends. When Duke Ellington gave a big concert in Paris in 1933, Josephine sent Pepito to the Duke's dressing room at the Salle Pleyel to invite him and his musicians to her performance the following afternoon at the Casino de Paris. Bricktop, who saw the performance, noticed that only Duke and a few others from the band attended. Why had not the others come? Josephine asked Bricktop. Whether fact or fiction, Bricktop replied, stories had "got around about how Josephine didn't want to see any colored people or have anything to do with them." The trouble seemed to be that whenever anybody went to see Josephine they had "to get by Pepito first, and he just turned them away." While denying she avoided people of her own race, Josephine had to admit that Pepito had never allowed her to see many people.

After a decade of success in Europe and South America, Pepito arranged for her debut in New York. He always arranged every detail so well. Josephine had some doubts about returning to New York, but since she had conquered the audiences in other countries, wouldn't the greatest triumph be found back where she started? She agreed to go, but the outcome was more than disappointing. In New York, despite Pepito's arrangements, which had always been so perfect elsewhere, nothing worked for her. She found that she was not the star performer there, not by a long shot, and the critics and the audiences did not respond as she expected them to do. She became furious with Pepito. They quarreled. In a fit of anger he took the next ship back to France, and Josephine never saw him again. By the time she returned to Paris, he was dead of cancer.

When Pepito died, everything Josephine thought belonged to her was tied up in his name. Buildings, a country chateau, expensive jewelry—all had been purchased in Pepito's name. "He told her," Bricktop recalled, "this was the thing to do, so that if anybody ever sued her for breach of contract, there wouldn't be anything they could get. As a matter of fact, she couldn't even draw five hundred francs at the box office, when she had her own show. Being dumb (or shall we say, in love with the guy, for I have known college bred ladies to do the same thing), she naturally did as he said. . . . It was a miracle she ever got anything. She had to go to law, but when they looked up Pepito's past and found he had never been in a position to buy such things, she got it all back—which certainly was lucky for her."

Except for New York, Josephine's success never seemed to falter during these years. She co-starred with Jean Gabin, one of France's greatest actors, in a film called *Zouzou*; she replaced the great Mistinguett as the star of the Casino de Paris; she played and sang the lead in Offenbach's *La Creole*; she appeared in a sumptuous charity gala before the president of France. Her stage opportunities were never ending and her cabaret made money, lots of money for her. But the money did not stick to her fingers. It somehow slipped away with great ease, as, alas, it has with so many stage stars.

And now she wanted something else. She wanted a baby, perhaps several babies. And so in 1937 she married Jean Lion, a rich industrialist. With this marriage she acquired French citizenship, and she embraced with fervor his Jewish faith, but she did not have a baby. Her body was not built for child-bearing. She was stunned by this disappointment. Her marriage drifted away after two or three years, and she and her husband were divorced.

When France declared war on Germany in September 1939, Josephine was co-starring at the Casino de Paris with Maurice Chevalier. When the show closed a few months later, she threw herself into war work with the same enthusiasm that she had given to the stage. She worked for the Resistance; she was made a lieutenant in the French Air Force; she entertained troops, both French and foreign Allies; and she became one of Charles de Gaulle's foremost backers, promoting his cause so that he would some day become the head of the French government when Germany was defeated and peace declared. She refused any compensation for her work, and she devoted herself to this effort night and day, even when her health was precarious. Besides high decorations—the Croix de Guerre, and the Legion of Honor with the Rosette of the Resistance—de Gaulle personally gave her a gold cross of Lorraine. It was her most prized jewel, though she later sold it at public auction to raise money for the Gaullist cause.

After the war, having lost all hope of having her own children, Josephine turned to an alternative idea, that of adopting four boys of different races and bringing them up together to show the world how happily people of different colored skins could live together on an equal mental and humanitarian basis.

And it was about this time that she renewed her friendship with Joseph Bouillon, a band leader she had known slightly ten years before. They were drawn together immediately because he, too, saw the importance of bringing together children of different races. They soon married and began the adoption of orphans of various nationalities, races and religions, whom Josephine would call her "Rainbow Tribe." It would be a noble experiment. On a three-hundred-acre estate she had purchased some years before in the Dordogne Valley in Southwestern France, she would house her children. To the ancient chateau, originally called "Les Mirandes" but which Josephine, who had always had difficulty negotiating her French "r," renamed "Les Milandes," would come visitors from all countries to view the happy results of her experiment. She told her plan to many of her friends, and some at least shared her enthusiasm for the project.

As the project moved forward Josephine's ideas also expanded. She had no understanding of the limitations of money. If a new idea pleased her she would go ahead with it without any financial planning, without any thought for the difficulties involved. Poor Bouillon! He didn't know what he was getting into, and he tried so hard to pull it off. But so often Josephine would embark on new or expanded plans without even telling him until her decision had been made and a commitment to others given. Very soon Josephine was in way over her head and was piling up an ever increasing financial burden.

As for the children, Josephine soon increased the original four to twelve, without consulting her husband in most cases, although the adoption, of course, had to have his consent. And of course they were all named Bouillon, and all became French citizens by their adoption. Josephine's "Rainbow Tribe" (they represented all colors) were babies put out for adoption or children that had been abandoned. There was a Korean; a very blond Finn; a French boy; a pure-blooded Indian from the highlands of Venezuela; a Japanese; a boy and girl found under a bush in Algeria, presumably Arabs; two black boys, one from the Coté d'Ivoire and one from Colombia; and a Jewish boy from Paris, since Israel would not let her adopt a male child. She encouraged each to learn his or her native language and ancestral religion— Buddhist, Shinto, Catholic, Jewish, Moslem—although in some cases it was difficult to find qualified teachers. Each was also encouraged to go back to his parental environment at least for a visit, if not for a couple of years' residence. This did not work out in most cases. The children were growing up in a French atmosphere, and inevitably they became more French than foreign. But her dream had come true. They were all happy together, very happy. She had shown that mixed races could indeed get along without friction. And they all loved Josephine and Jo Bouillon, Mama and Papa, as they were called.

And then Josephine added another dimension to her original plan. She wanted "Les Milandes" to become a College of Brotherhood, a coordinating point for the study of ways to abolish the prejudices of race, religion, and social class—a grandiose scheme in which many countries would participate, sending their students and their teachers, and building a movement that would change the world. Italy, Morocco, and Yugoslavia promised to cooperate. The countries themselves would provide the necessary money, and she would give the land, her beloved "Les Milandes" in the Dordogne.

In the meantime, her financial affairs were not going at all well. Creditors constantly threatened to seize and sell "Les Milandes" to pay their accounts. Josephine would not herself beg for money to save the estate, but she was quite happy to have Jo Bouillon do it for her. She even arranged an interview with de Gaulle, but then sent Jo to the meeting in her place. Not a few plans were suggested, some of them quite feasible, but in the end Josephine refused them all. One of the best was to make a full-length film of her life and of the "Rainbow Tribe," showing how her children lived together in peace and happiness, but again, at the last moment, she turned this down because she "could not stand to exploit her children." Bouillon must have wondered if she really wanted to save "Les Milandes."

It was at this stage that she sent her husband to the American ambassador in Paris to see what the American government would do for her College of Brotherhood, and the matter was turned over to me to handle. I liked Jo Bouillon very much. He was so sincere, so earnest, so passionate in his devotion to Josephine and her desire to promote world brotherhood. But there was nothing I could do. It was not the kind of project which would fit into Washington's idea of aid to education.

Josephine did not come to see me herself at that time, but she did come on another occasion. This was during a visit to Paris by a group of sixty American black women lawyers and law clerks, which was sponsored by the Department of State. I was told to "do something" for them, so I arranged a reception in the gardens of the Embassy, and I asked Josephine if she would attend. She accepted immediately, on short notice. We spent a delightful couple of hours that afternoon. She talked to them as a group about her College of Brotherhood and then chatted with them individually. She spoke seriously and she handled herself with great poise and sincerity. Everyone was impressed. What I had feared might be a rather dull gathering had turned into the highlight of the European tour of my guests and a memorable afternoon for me and the other Embassy staff present.

In 1969 "Les Milandes" and her belongings were sold at auction. Josephine had to be carried from her chateau by gendarmes. The new owners locked it up and left it to decay, as I discovered on a visit there a few years later. When the "Rainbow Tribe" and their parents were forced out of their home, the children were brought to Paris, where they lived in very crowded conditions. They later went on to Monte Carlo, where Princess Grace gave them a proper place to live and other assistance. In time they grew up and now have gone their separate ways, but they always retained their close ties to Mama and Papa and to each other.

Josephine and her husband separated, too, but they were never divorced, and they always remained closely attached to the "Rainbow Tribe." Josephine died suddenly in April 1975, only two days after opening a new revue celebrating her fifty years as an entertainer. Her last triumph showed once again that she could never become a has-been in the theatrical world.

Hadley Hemingway

THE best-liked woman in Montparnasse was probably Ernest Hemingway's first wife, Hadley. All other women and many men seemed to have liked her. I suspect it was a low-key attachment stemming from her sterling qualities that drew people to her. She was a devoted wife and mother, an economical housekeeper, and a boon companion for her husband in whatever adventures he chose to pursue. Despite all these high-sounding virtues, she was fun to talk to, an interesting person once you got beyond her initial shyness. Some of the men, of course, found her a little dull because she would not flirt with them, but they did not really hold it against her. In a community where gossip was rampant, no one included Hadley in their whispers. Hadley was a tall girl with auburn hair, a somewhat bony figure, and large warm eyes. You might not particularly notice her in a group of people, but once you talked to her and felt her magnetism, you did not easily forget her.

Hadley had one important thing to give her husband even before their marriage, when most of their courting was done by mail: a steadfast and absolute belief in his ability to write and an assurance that publishers as well as the public would soon recognize his work. Her faith was not built on any innate literary sense that she possessed, but rather on her great love for Ernest. To foster his career she worked very hard; she urged him to drop journalism and any outside work and devote himself entirely to his writing. This would not have been possible had she not had a small, very small, income from a trust fund. Still, it was enough to eke out an unencumbered existence in the most modest circumstances of Montparnasse life.

Fortunately, the necessities of life were cheap in Paris in the early twenties. The Hemingways lived in a tiny two-room apartment in the rue Cardinal Lemoine, a workingman's district near a public market where rents were low and food was cheap and plentiful. The district at that time was not a tough or

Hadley Hemingway and Ernest, on a walking tour in the Black Forest, Germany, 1922 (*Photo courtesy of John Hadley Nicanor Hemingway*).

dangerous one, as some biographers have stated, but a community of kindly, simple people, honest and friendly.

For Hadley this life had great benefits. She had been brought up by a dominating mother and sister, who repeatedly told her she was a sickly young woman who must be sheltered from the world. They discouraged companionship with men and women of her own age. Giving in to their injunctions, she grew up deprived of the opportunities to develop a sense of self-confidence; she was afraid of the world, afraid of the outsiders. But Hem, as he was called in those days, changed all this. He made friends easily and inspired confidence in others. Hadley gradually came out of her cocoon, began to feel comfortable with the writers and artists and others she met in Montparnasse as well as with the working people around her. She learned to speak French and slowly made many friends among the French writers and painters, too. This new world was very exciting for Hadley and she enjoyed every minute of it. Although she was eight years older than Hem, she was in many ways less mature than her husband, and from him she learned a great deal about life. For his part he loved to instruct her as much as he enjoyed instructing those of his friends, such as Sylvia Beach and Adrienne Monnier, who were interested or amused by his display of knowledge.

And even in their poverty, Hem and Hadley were able to take occasional trips to Switzerland, Italy, and Spain, always riding third class on the trains and putting up at the most modest inns, ski lodges, and pensions.

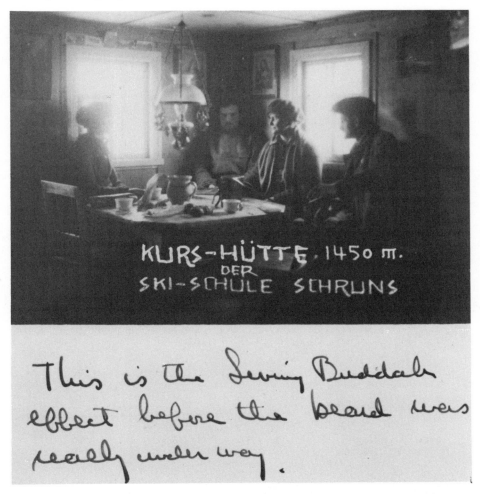

KURS-HÜTTE. 1450 m.
DER
SKI-SCHULE SCHRUNS

This is the Living Buddah effect before the beard was really under way.

Hadley Hemingway with Ernest (center), Schruns, Austria, mid-1920s. Caption in Hemingway's writing reads: "This is the Living Buddah effect before the beard was really under way" (*Photo from the papers of Sylvia Beach, Princeton University Library*).

When their son came along, John Hadley Nicanor Hemingway, who was at once nicknamed Bumby (a name that stuck to him until he was in his teens and became Jack to his friends), Hadley gave herself to motherhood with the same devotion she had given to matrimony. Bumby had been born in Toronto while Hem was working as a journalist there. Both parents wanted their child to be born on American soil and had left Paris three months before he was born. Things did not go well in Toronto, however, and the family soon returned to Paris, where they found an apartment next to a sawmill in the rue Notre Dame des Champs, a fine street close to the Luxembourg Gardens. Life

Ernest and Hadley Hemingway, Schruns, Austria, 1925–26 (Photo courtesy of John Hadley Nicanor Hemingway).

in the new apartment began to change in style for both of them. Hem was beginning to have a little reputation. Other writers were starting to take him seriously. Hadley was very happy with these changes. Her social life was enlarged, she met more and more interesting people, and they were frequently invited to dinners and parties they both found stimulating and enjoyable. They still had very little money, but they were already tasting the good things of life with no obligation to reciprocate.

And then there appeared on the scene someone who quickly decided that

Hemingway was for her and that she would get him away from Hadley. Her name was Pauline Pfeiffer, a fashion writer working in Paris for *Vogue* magazine. The only thing Hadley and Pauline had in common was Saint Louis, where both had grown up, though each without knowing that the other existed. Pauline was four years younger than Hadley and was everything that Hadley was not—small, petite, elegantly dressed as though she had just stepped out of the pages of *Vogue,* as indeed she had. She was "smooth" in the expression of the day, superficially knowledgeable if not highly educated, beautifully mannered, feminine, never aggressive in her approach to others, yet her presence was always felt. By comparison, poor Hadley looked gauche and uncertain. Hadley's sterling qualities did not show on the surface, and being shy and still somewhat unsure of herself, she made little effort to put her best foot forward. She had probably never been in competition with another woman before. It was not her game.

Hem may have felt, consciously or not, that marriage to Pauline would bring him certain material advantages which he had not previously enjoyed. He was undoubtedly tired of being poor. He knew that even a successful writer did not earn large sums as a rule. Pauline had an income of her own, and her relatives were mostly rather wealthy, especially her bachelor uncle, Gus Pfeiffer, a very successful New York businessman, who doted on his neice.

John Dos Passos, Sara Murphy, Hadley Hemingway, (behind) Ernest Hemingway and Gerald Murphy, Schruns, Austria, 1925–26 *(Photo courtesy of John Hadley Nicanor Hemingway).*

Hadley Hemingway with vine leaves in her hair, 1923 (*Photo courtesy of John Hadley Nicanor Hemingway*).

After her marriage to Hemingway, it was he who gave them the house in Key West and financed the safari in Africa and the deep sea fishing excursions in the Caribbean. Pauline paid for the five servants that manned the Florida establishment. This was quite a change from the two-room apartment in the rue Cardinal Lemoine.

Hadley helped to make Hemingway a writer, and Pauline made "Papa," as he was beginning to be called around this time, a big-game hunter. He wrote very little while he was living with her.

It just happened that I had lunch with Pauline about the time she was developing her campaign to win Hemingway for herself. We were both guests of her *Vogue* colleagues, Eric and Lee Erickson, a charming couple. During the meal Pauline confessed that she was indeed determined to capture Ernest's love if she could, and it was evident that she was going about it with the skill and persistence of a born hunter. When I asked her if she thought Hadley would mind her activity, she merely looked at me with undisguised scorn and shrugged her shoulders. After she had left, the Ericksons and I decided she was a most dangerous woman. Many others shared this view, but no one, as far as I know, had the courage to tell this to Hem. If anyone did, he was probably brutally rebuffed as an interfering outsider.

Pauline attached herself to the Hemingways, made great pretenses of friendship for Hadley, went on vacations with them, and bought small gifts for them, especially for Hadley. Then when Hemingway was finally seriously attracted to her, Hadley was told that she might lose her husband. She was appalled, dismayed, and terribly hurt for a while. At first she resisted the idea, asked for time, but in the end accepted the separation and subsequent divorce with surprising equanimity. After all, she said later, "They were in love."

Speculation on the right and wrong of such separations never proves anything, but it is my belief that this was, in the long run, the best possible thing for Hadley. She would not have enjoyed life with Hemingway in the successful years, I fear, or in the years when his paranoia became more and more pronounced. Following their divorce in January 1927, Hadley felt as though she had been "released." "I didn't know," she recalled later, "what was going to happen to me, but I had lots of confidence in myself and plenty of friends both at home and abroad. I knew that I could get along, and I knew that I could still get some fun out of music. And we divided Bumby."

I want to go back for a moment to the years when Hem was still struggling with the dual life of working as a journalist and trying to write at the same time. We were both members—junior members—of the Anglo-American Press Association of Paris, a group of fifteen to twenty newspapermen who gathered on Wednesdays for lunch. This was a congenial group, experienced, knowledgeable foreign correspondents, mostly well established in their careers. Several of them took a certain interest in Hemingway as a writer, notably Bill Bird, who as a hobby operated a little press he called Three Mountains. It was Bird who printed by hand Hemingway's book *In Our Time*.

The members all liked Hem and often helped him with his journalistic work if they could. They continued to see him even after he ceased to be active in the newspaper field. Among the top correspondents of this group was a man named Paul Scott Mowrer, the European correspondent for the *Chicago Daily News* and definitely a giant in our midst. Like the rest of us, Hem looked up to him as a shrewd political observer, a skilled writer, and a warmhearted friend. But we were also a little in awe of him.

Of course Hem told Hadley about the men he met at the Wednesday meetings, but there was no opportunity for her to meet any of them unless they became personal friends outside of the journalistic fraternity. She admired them from a distance, especially Paul Scott Mowrer, whom she finally met in the spring of 1927, just after her divorce from Hemingway had become final. By this time, Hadley had developed the gifts she had received from Ernest. She was more mature and had a quiet self-assurance. And so with Paul Mowrer, who was then a widower, she found a new life, and a lasting happiness. In 1933 they married. Hadley had the good fortune to make a wonderful life for herself in two quite different worlds. The few years with Hem would always bear the enchantment of newness and discovery. From him she received the "key to the world."

Nadia Boulanger

IF asked to name the person who has made the greatest contribution to American music in the twentieth century, most musicians would probably pick Nadia Boulanger. Though she was not a resident of Montparnasse, most of the young Left Bank composers flocked to her apartment on the hill of Montmartre overlooking the city. This intense, erect, vigorous brunette, with the soft, yet vibrant voice, was the catalytic agent who would give to innumerable American composers the basic musical training for their creative efforts. No one who met Nadia Boulanger could ever forget her burning ardor to achieve perfection in the works of her pupils, her unwillingness to accept anything less.

Nadia was "discovered" almost at the same time by three Americans who arrived at her door by different routes in 1921. One was Virgil Thomson, who later gave us some of our best church music and also the musical score for Gertrude Stein's *Four Saints in Three Acts,* and who, for so many years, was the gifted music critic of the *New York Herald Tribune.* Another important youthful composer was Aaron Copland, who has provided a lifetime of fascinating popular songs, ballets, and orchestral pieces. The third of this trio was Melville Smith, who later headed the Longy School of Music in Cambridge, Massachusetts. Through these three, word soon got around that if you wanted to study music seriously, creatively, at the "graduate" level, you had to go to Paris to study with La Boulanger.

Students came in large numbers, and among them were such future giants as Walter Piston, Herbert Elwell, Roy Harris, Marc Blitzstein, Theodore Chanler, Elliott Carter, and Paul Bowles. Nadia had a very special interest in her American students because she felt that we were entering an era of great musical productivity, as indeed we were, and as the Russians had done in the 1840s. To dramatize her belief, she organized, in 1926, a concert at the Salle

53

Nadia Boulanger, music teacher and friend to American composers, Paris, about 1921 *(Photo courtesy of Madame Annette Dieudonne).*

Gaveau devoted entirely to the works of her American students. Though he had not studied with her, the then popular composer George Antheil also appeared on the program, thanks to Virgil Thomson, who petitioned Nadia to include him.

Nadia was a warm, friendly person who, Aaron Copland noticed, possessed a "womanliness that seemed quite unaware of its own charm." She lived the lives of her pupils, demanding that they work ("No student ever arrived late for his appointment a second time") and enjoying their success as much as they did. She remained a friend to each of them for the rest of their lives, and they were and remain devoted to her.

Nadia came from a long line of musicians. Her grandfather was an opera singer, as was her Russian mother, born Princess Mytchetsky, a jolly, roly-poly woman who had also been an opera singer. Her father was a composer and professor at the Conservatoire National de Paris. Her sister, Lili, was also a gifted composer, the first woman to win the coveted Prix de Rome in music. Sadly, Lili came to an untimely death in 1918 from tuberculosis. But her music lives on and is played in many countries today. Nadia was also a composer but she decided that her greatest talent lay in teaching, which she continued doing until her death in 1979 at the age of ninety-two.

Virgil Thomson has told how she sat down at the piano with each pupil and went over his latest compositions note by note, discussing, analyzing, suggesting changes, pointing out weak passages and good portions. And Aaron Copland has remembered her "consuming need" to discover how all music functions, her vast technical knowledge, and her ability to impart to her students a sense of confidence. She could locate the flaws in a composer's work before it was finished and tell him why they were flaws. Often she would play his music, for she had a phenomenal ability as a sight reader. Above all, the pupil always felt her deep personal interest in his work, and this became both an education and an inspiration. But no matter how much she insisted on the perfection of technique, she was very careful not to influence his creative ideas. These must be purely his own, or they were valueless.

On Wednesday afternoon she would invite a number of her pupils to her fourth floor apartment at 36 rue Ballu, now changed to 3 Lili Boulanger. Up to the time of her death it remained as it was in 1921, a crowded living room with two concert grand pianos and a full-sized church organ as well as an assemblage of that peculiar furniture that marked the 1900s in France, not the most beautiful, but sturdy and useful. On the mantlepiece stood a marble bust of her sister and over it a madonna, for Nadia was a devout Catholic. In politics she was a Royalist and thus part of a small and ineffectual party headed by the astute and cultured comte de Paris. The pupils sat around her, discussing the music of various periods from pre-Bach to post-Stravinsky—for her interest in music extended from ancient to classical to ultramodern—always analyzing, trying to extract that essence which would be useful in their own creations. Every composer must be a musician and every musician must have had some experience as a composer: that was Nadia's firm belief, and one she had practiced herself. After these discussions Nadia would serve tea and cakes, very good cakes, indeed, for I myself have had some, though I was never a pupil of hers.

Nadia worked long hours at her teaching. Her first pupil might arrive as early as seven in the morning, and the last might come at midnight. In addition to her private pupils, she played the organ at the church of La Madeleine, noted for its great music. She also taught at the Conservatoire and in the summer at the American Conservatory in a wing of that chateau at Fountainebleau. This school for American students was founded in 1921 by Walter Damrosch. She made her first American tour in 1925, performing among other compositions Copland's Symphony for Organ and Orchestra, a work she had coaxed from her student in the months prior to her tour. She was the first woman to conduct the Boston Symphony Orchestra, the New York Philharmonic, the Philadelphia and Washington Symphony orchestras, and the Royal Philharmonic of London, a notable achievement, for it marked the end of male dominence in the music world. She also taught and lectured at many colleges and universities, such as Radcliffe and Wellesley, Juilliard and Longy. In later years many honors were heaped upon her by governments and academic institutions including honorary doctorates from Harvard, Smith, Brown, and Oxford, and awards from the governments of France and Poland.

When Nadia turned eighty, many of her admirers and former students gathered to celebrate her birthday. Prince Rainier and Princess Grace of Monaco gave a beautiful concert and reception in her honor in Monte Carlo to which my wife and I were invited. It was an evening to remember with many of the world's greatest musicians and distinguished personalities packed into that lovely little theater on the hill overlooking the bay. The program included one of Lili's compositions and many of Nadia's favorite pieces. At the end the violinist Yehudi Menuhin, a former student of Nadia's, played "Happy Birthday" while the audience rose and sang with all eyes fixed on Nadia standing in the royal box alongside the prince and the princess. It was a moving spectacle in that fairy-tale setting.

In addition to all her associations with American students, musicians and institutions in the United States, Nadia had a devoted group of friends around her in Paris, such as Igor Stravinsky and Arnold Schönberg, whose works she greatly admired; Maurice Ravel, who had been a classmate of hers at the Conservatoire; and the writers Paul Claudel and Paul Valéry, both important members of her circle. Among her French students were such notables as Francis Poulenc and the late Darius Milhaud, who also gave so much to America.

Besides her teaching, Nadia had one other passion in life, the perpetuation of the memory of her sister Lili and her music. Lili had died on the fifteenth of March 1918 at the age of twenty-five. Most of her compositions were written in the last five years of her life when she was already seriously ill. Nadia and her mother nursed her with loving care, but the doctors could not stop the progress of the disease. After Lili's death, Nadia and her mother decided to set aside the month of March each year as a period of mourning and meditation. Nadia withdrew during that time from all social activity except her teaching. And each year, on or about March 15, Nadia arranged for a memorial service to be held in the church of La Trinité, consisting largely of the performance of some of Lili's religious music. I attended three of these memorial services along with two or three hundred devoted friends of Nadia.

It was a beautiful two-and-a-half-hour service, taking most of the afternoon. Lili's music is very impressive. Through Nadia and through her good friend the Marquise Yvonne de Casa Fuerte, I met many of the people who attended these services, musicians all, mostly French but with a scattering of Americans and British, and all devoted to the music of Lili. Although Nadia is gone, these annual memorial services are still held today, I am told. All those who attended were deeply devoted to Nadia, to the point where tears would come in the eyes of some during the service. "She is a great woman," they would say, "a truly remarkable individual."

Zelda Fitzgerald

ZELDA, the wife of F. Scott Fitzgerald, was undoubtedly the most attractive woman in Montparnasse. One was struck at once by her wideset, deep blue eyes that were warm and always laughing with you, her perfectly formed figure, her marvelously clean and pure complexion, her agreeable Southern accent that was soft and soothing. But none of this would have carried her very far had it not been for the animation, the humor, the flirtatiousness which she brought to every occasion. She flirted obviously and wholeheartedly with every man she met, but only a few failed to understand, and very quickly, that this was not a come-on. For Zelda, flirting was a way of making conversation, and I must say a very agreeable one. There were, however, two men who did not understand this, Ernest Hemingway and her husband Scott.

Hemingway met her about the same time I did, I believe, sometime during the summer of 1925. Hemingway, with so many fine traits of mind and character, tended to be a little overserious, and although he at first professed to admire Zelda, he turned against her when he found out that Zelda with all her flirtatiousness was not ready to jump into his arms. In Scott's case her flirting brought on a stupid jealousy which rose like a black cloud in front of him and caused him to quarrel with her. As in so many instances of jealousy, there was absolutely no grounds for Scott's attitude, but no jealousy is based on reason. From all evidence, Zelda's affection for him never strayed during her entire life, even after he abandoned her.

But Zelda had other attractive traits. She was a beautiful dancer although she never became a creditable ballet performer. She could also sing with a certain amount of talent that was never fully developed. She painted in several media, and she sculped. And, of course, she wrote short stories that compared favorably with those of Scott. Her one novel, the largely autobiographical *Save*

57

Zelda Fitzgerald with Scott, seated on runningboard of their Marmon, Montgomery, Alabama, 1920 *(Photo from the papers of F. Scott Fitzgerald, Princeton University Library)*.

Me the Waltz, shows that she had a real talent which might have been outstanding if she had been allowed to develop it. Had Scott been more understanding, more intelligent about her, the two would have made a wonderful literary team, in my opinion. Basically, Scott was a very decent, generous, likable, friendly man—when sober. But drunk, he could be unbearable, abusive, cruel, and vile-mouthed.

Zelda and Scott came from very different backgrounds. Zelda was a Southern belle of the story books, a Gibson Girl type, a young lady who never went to college but became the recognized queen of all the campuses of Alabama and surrounding states in the years from 1917 to 1920. Her beaux were legion. She lived in Montgomery, the old capital of the Confederacy with its proud traditions, where her father was a judge of the Alabama Supreme Court from 1909 to 1931, a dignified and respected pillar of society. Zelda was a little "wild," but everyone said she would "soon marry and settle down."

Scott, on the other hand, had no family tradition to point to. He came from Saint Paul, Minnesota, where his father was a salesman with little money. He also spent part of his youth in New Jersey. There he managed to talk his way into Princeton after an initial rejection, and he came perilously close to flunking out once he got in, but World War I came along and Scott found himself in a military camp in Montgomery, a second lieutenant in the U.S. Army. Here he met Zelda, then only seventeen.

Scott and Zelda had little in common, yet the one passion they did share was very strong indeed. They were both "excitement-eaters," a phrase that Zelda used in her book to describe herself. Gerald Murphy, a close friend, later observed that the Fitzgeralds did not seek ordinary pleasures. They wanted something unusual to happen, some act that they might not even understand. Zelda had never seen a young man who loved excitement, antics, outrageous happenings as much as she did, perhaps more. It was the thing that caused her to choose Scoot as a husband over all the highly eligible suitors of the good old South. She was also attracted to him because he was a writer and already successful before their marriage in the rectory of Saint Patrick's Cathedral in New York in April 1920. She was almost twenty and he twenty-three. It was a quiet wedding without flowers or fanfare conducted in the presence of one of her sisters. For the next ten years they were the most renowned "excitement-eaters" of the Western world.

But Scott was jealous of any effort at self-expression that Zelda might exert. He wanted it all for himself, I fear, but then he failed to develop his own talents to their highest.

Hemingway used to say that Zelda prevented Scott from working on his writing. He was also supposed to have told Scott that Zelda was crazy. Zelda, to Scott's dismay, thought Hemingway was "bogus." It was writing, however, that formed and animated the friendship between the two men. For Hemingway, a dedicated but unknown writer in 1925, the author of *The Great Gatsby* was a curiosity. Hemingway worked very hard at his own writing, very hard

Zelda Fitzgerald, with daughter Scottie and Scott, Rome, 1924 *(Photo from the papers of F. Scott Fitzgerald, Princeton University Library).*

indeed, and he thought that any writer must work just as hard or his writing would not be good. Such purity and total dedication to writing impressed Scott. But Zelda did not stop Scott from working, really. There were several reasons why Scott found it difficult to concentrate on his work. One was that he was easily affected by alcohol so that a quiet little drinking bout usually turned into a week-long binge that left him spent and exhausted physically and mentally, while Hemingway, who really drank very little despite his boasting about his capacity, was not seriously affected by alcohol and usually felt fine after a night's sleep, ready to put in a good six hours of concentrated effort with pen and paper.

But the most important obstacle for Scott was that Zelda, unlike Hadley Hemingway, did not stay home with the baby, but instead went out on her own, alone, to find a little fun if Scott was working. To Hadley, Zelda seemed charming and lovely but also frivolous and at times canny. Once Zelda remarked to Hadley that it seemed that Ernest directed everything in the Hemingway family. Obviously, it would not be that way in the Fitzgerald household. As soon as Zelda was gone, Scott began to worry about her. Where was she? Was she with other men? His jealousy rose before his eyes once again. So he went to find her and his writing was put off for another week or two. If there was going to be any excitement-eating, Scott wanted to be in on the feast, though Scott's version was often less humorous than Zelda's and sometimes more brutal. Both loved these carryings-on—what Hemingway called the "festival conception of life"—and both loved the publicity which often followed them wherever they went in Europe or in the United States. In that sense they were made for each other.

It was at the Dingo that I saw them most often and it was there that they met Hemingway also. The Fitzgeralds used the Dingo as a taking off place for their frequent forages in the nightclubs, or sometimes they would go off to private parties of their rich friends. Compared to the rest of us, Scott was rich, but he and Zelda had no sense of money whatsoever. It went through their hands like water, and if they ran out of it they lived just as high on credit, which was always available to such prodigal spenders. They often invited Hem and myself to join them in Montmartre, at their expense, of course, because they were always very generous with their friends, but I never went because I did not like to have someone paying for me, and I could not afford to go on my own, or at least not in the lavish way they operated. Hemingway had the same feeling, and I believe he never went either, certainly not in those years. Anyway, he really did not care for the Montmartre night life, at least in the years I knew him best.

One night my wife and I were sitting with Zelda and Scott at a table in the Dingo. They were having one of their not infrequent quarrels. Scott was a little drunk, and he was accusing Zelda of "carrying on" with some man who had been in the bar a little earlier. Finally, he said to her, "You bitch!" That pushed my chivalry button. I jumped up and said, "Scott, you can't call Zelda a bitch. I won't stand for it." He rose, too, and I landed my fist squarely on his

Zelda Fitzgerald, traveling in Provence, autumn, 1929. In the background is the Maison Carrée, Nîmes *(Photo from the papers of F. Scott Fitzgerald, Princeton University Library).*

jaw. It was not a hard blow. It did not hurt him, I think. But I must have caught him off balance, for he collapsed to the floor in a heap, like a discarded raincoat. Jimmy the Barman rushed over to "separate" us, but I had already backed away, rather appalled by what I had done. Jimmy helped him up, brushed off his immaculate suit, and put him down at a vacant table nearby. He brought him a new drink, and I returned to our table. Zelda said nothing then, but a few minutes later she said, "I'd better go over and talk to him." She did, and a short time after they left without a word to us.

I did not see Scott for several days, but when I ran into him again at the Dingo I immediately told him how sorry I was for the incident the other evening. "It's all right," he said with pleasant warmth in his voice. We shook hands, and I bought him a drink.

On another occasion when Zelda had an argument with Scott, she turned to me and said, "I wish you would hit him again. He needs it." Scott looked up rather startled, but Zelda and I laughed, and he did too.

But Zelda wanted a lot more than simply to be the wife of a famous writer. She wanted to be known as a writer herself. In the winter of 1928–29, she started work on six stories about young women, which *College Humor* had agreed to publish if they bore the signatures of both Scott and Zelda. Although the stories attracted attention, they are lifeless descriptions of fashionable girls whose *beau monde* existence seems contrived and detached. They seem to suffer what Zelda herself exhibited: an inability to overcome boredom and attach herself to something tangible. Zelda wanted to be recognized for her own abilities and this is probably the reason why, in addition to the writing, she took up the ballet, a particularly feminine art in which Scott was unlikely to compete. Her competitiveness is best seen in *Save Me the Waltz*, which she wrote in 1931–32 when she had been, for at least part of the time, in mental hospitals in Switzerland and Baltimore. It is a most interesting book, an impressionistic treatment of so-called expatriate life in Europe in the twenties that is in sharp contrast to the traditional life in the deep South as she had known it as a child and as it still existed in the thirties. It is an interesting book, too, because it reveals so much of Zelda's impassioned desire for success, and especially what she hoped would come from her dancing. "It seemed to Alabama [the heroine's name suggests the many autobiographical associations with Zelda] that, reaching her goal, she would drive the devils that had driven her—that, in proving herself, she would achieve that peace which she imagined went only in surety of one's self—that she would be able, through the medium of the dance, to command her emotions, to summon love or pity or happiness at will, having provided a channel through which they might flow. She drove herself mercilessly."*

Zelda submitted the manuscript of her novel directly to Max Perkins, the editor in chief of Scribner's, with a request that it not be shown to Scott, but Perkins could not bring himself to publish it without showing it to the husband

*Zelda Fitzgerald. *Save Me the Waltz*. (Carbondale, Ill.: Southern Illinois University Press, 1967),

of the writer. Scott blew his top. He considered that many parts of the book were insulting to him, injurious to his reputation and a theft of his own literary ideas. He insisted that the manuscript be extensively revised. At first Zelda refused, but later agreed to make the changes under pressure from both Perkins and Scott. It is unfortunate that the original text has been lost, perhaps deliberately destroyed, so that the extent of the cuts and changes demanded by Scott will never be known. After reading the final text, one can easily see why some of the changes were made. For instance, the name of the "hero" was changed from Amory Blaine, the name of the hero of *This Side of Paradise,* to David Knight. That was not a change in text, of course, but an effort to dissociate Zelda as a writer from her husband. It is also clear that the character and the actions attributed to David have been watered down to the point that he becomes an unreal character even though he appears on every other page, the polite, generous man, kind and considerate for the most part, especially in the last half of the book, whereas Scott was in real life anything but this amiable character. It is, on the other hand, Zelda who comes alive under the name of Alabama. Zelda worked very hard to find success in ballet, and in the story Alabama did indeed find such success. The change is an example of wishful thinking on Zelda's part, for as a close friend of hers at this time recently noted, Zelda showed little promise as a dancer, partly because she started her studies too late. It was a bitter pill to swallow.

By the time she wrote this book, Zelda had changed her life-style rather drastically. She no longer drank as she had in the twenties; partying bored her; small talk she found dull. She had become a serious and often strangely silent young woman, while Scott continued to live in the Jazz Age that they had once created. A doctor at Shepherd-Pratt, in Baltimore, told Scott what I have always believed, that it was he who needed psychiatric treatment, not Zelda. The remark infuriated him. This opinion was also shared by one of Zelda's close friends who was with her in the Highland Psychiatric Hospital in Asheville, North Carolina. Zelda, she told me, was very popular with the people in the mental institutions she lived in, and although she did some erratic things, she was not in any way unbalanced.

Zelda was doing her best "to take what she wanted when she could," a conviction she attributes to Alabama. But as relentless as she was, she failed to attain the ends she really desired: some sort of financial independence from Scott; a life of her own in which she could develop her own abilities without Scott telling her what to do. She remained dependent on Scott, however, both financially and morally. She had been dominated by him over too long a period, and she had no experience of fending for herself. So in the end she went back to her family in Montgomery to be enfolded once again in the warmth of the old South, to take up her old religion, to be cared for by the people who know her best, the folk of her childhood. What a loss!

Perkins published her novel, but even though it had some good reviews, it failed to catch the public eye, partly perhaps because Scribner's did not give it any serious promotion. Also, no doubt because her type of writing, which had been so successful in the twenties, had lost its appeal for the general public. Scott saw less and less of her. He had virtually abandoned her, although he gave her a modest financial allowance. He continued his effort to drink up all the liquor in America, established himself with the journalist Sheilah Graham, and eventually died of a heart attack in Encino, in the San Fernando Valley, on December 21, 1941. He was forty-five years old.

Zelda meanwhile lived quietly with her mother in Montgomery, not however as a recluse, as some have stated. Parties, drinking, excitement-eating were gone forever, and now she devoted herself to painting, some dancing, and friendship with those around her. Her bitterness toward Scott soon changed to affection for him once again, and she wrote him loving letters, though his liaison with Miss Graham had hurt her deeply. She was not in good health, however, and was unable to attend his funeral in Rockville, Maryland. After his death she played the role of the widow in all seriousness.

When her mental balance was not on the even keel she desired, she would return to the Highland Psychiatric Hospital in Asheville for treatment. Ashe-

ville always remained Zelda's refuge. Although the director of the hospital, Dr. Robert Carroll, enforced a regimen that excluded medicine and forbade the wearing of all cosmetics and required regular chapel attendance every Sunday afternoon, the physical program he had designed for his patients exhilarated her. She welcomed the pleasantly exhausting demands of hiking, picnicing, walking, and sports like tennis. One of her tennis partners remembered that Zelda retained all her competitive spirit on the courts. She simply had to win, and on the rare occasions when she lost, she invariably snapped her racket in two. Scott's visits to Asheville, sometimes with their daughter Scottie, sometimes alone, were usually brief. He stayed at the expensive Grove Park Inn, a few blocks from the hospital, but one who saw him in Asheville remembered he never took his wife to dine at the inn. Around the hospital he struck a pose of superiority and strutted about as though conscious of his handsome good looks. Beneath the outward charm, it seemed, there was an arrogant strain.

At Highland, Zelda went on with her painting, working alongside other patients in a large studio and turning out a series of "dream fantasies." One who often saw her paintings observed Zelda's remarkable color sense and the literal quality of another series, her "flower" paintings, with their attractive arrangements and colors, so distinct from the "dream" pictures that depended on distortion for their effect.

From "real" life Zelda often seemed to disappear, a friend who was with her at Highland has observed. It was almost as though she vanished bodily into a cloud, a rapturous cloud, detaching herself from everyone and everything. Also, at times, she would talk to no one in particular, addressing her remarks to space, as though she were on stage. But when she spoke directly to someone, one had to listen and respond. She conveyed the feeling that she expected people to keep up with her.

She was living at Highland on March 10, 1948, when, late at night, fire broke out. In a short time the whole building was in flames. Zelda was on the third floor, and because of locked doors and barred windows, she was unable to get out. The fire was too strong to permit the fireman to reach her and ten other patients. Her charred remains were buried alongside the body of her husband. A single stone marks the two graves with the inscription: FRANCIS SCOTT KEY FITZGERALD AND HIS WIFE, ZELDA.

Zelda Fitzgerald and Scott attending the theater, Baltimore, 1932 *(Photo from Cornell University Library).*

Peggy Guggenheim

THE life of a patron of the arts is not an easy one, as Peggy Guggenheim found out early in her life. She was a warmhearted, generous person who embraced the arts, poetry, writing, and intellectual pursuits without herself having any talents in any of them. All she had was money, lots of it, some people said. Her first husband, Laurence Vail, once quipped that when any problem arose Peggy's first instinct was to reach for her checkbook. Laurence lived off an allowance of one hundred dollars a month, and Peggy's yearly income averaged around twenty-three thousand dollars. These remarks are utterly unfair, or at least grossly exaggerated, yet money, of which she had plenty indeed, played an important role in the life she led in Montparnasse.

Peggy was born in 1898 to a family of rich Jewish bourgeoisie. They gave her maximum indulgence and minimum education; she brushed aside the idea of college. At fourteen she lost her father who went down on the ill-fated maiden voyage of the *Titanic*. Her mother, Florette, was saved, and for the rest of her life, she remained devoted to her three daughters, Marguerite (Peggy), Benita, and Hazel. Peggy's sisters were beauties, but she, although very attractive with her chestnut hair and green eyes, had an unfortunate nose which caused her considerable anguish. A plastic surgeon in Cincinnati once attempted to give her a new nose, but the operation failed, and after a painful recuperation she had to live with a nose that remained much as it was before.

Once out of school Peggy took a couple of minor jobs, the most interesting of which was with her cousin, Harold Loeb, who himself was to become a figure in Montparnasse in future years. At that time he ran a bookshop near Grand Central Station called the Sunwise Turn, a place considered "radical" by some. There, as his shop assistant, Peggy met many prominent writers and

Peggy Guggenheim with her son Sindbad and daughter Pegeen, 1934 *(Photo courtesy of Sindbad Vail).*

had her first taste of the literary world. She also sold yards of books to her unliterary aunts who used them to fill up their empty bookcases. Even during these early years, Peggy was drawn to the avant-garde. Margaret Anderson, in New York to publish installments of James Joyce's *Ulysses* in her little magazine, *The Little Review*, persuaded Peggy to donate five hundred dollars for an issue of the magazine on the grounds that by doing so she would be helping "to prevent a new war by dedicating herself to the arts."

The Guggenheims traveled to Europe frequently, and, unsurprisingly, they always stayed in the most posh hotels. It was while in Paris in 1923 that Peggy met a man who introduced her to a side of life she had never dreamed existed. His name was Laurence Vail, an American, then twenty-nine, who had been brought up in Europe and knew all the ins and outs of the "good life" on the Continent. Vail's father and mother lived in Europe, too, as did his sister, Clotilde. His father was a painter, half Breton French, half American. His sister was a singer. Laurence himself was a writer of considerable talent but no great perseverance or perspective. He knew the rich art world of Paris in those years, though, and he introduced Peggy to dozens of painters of various nationalities, many of whom would later become world famous. Laurence liked to call his friends "bohemians," and he himself was known as the "king of Bohemia." Peggy embraced their life-style with all the enthusiasm of a child who has just discovered candy. Above all, Laurence enthralled her. "He

appeared to me like someone out of another world,", she wrote in her autobiography.

> He was the first man I knew who never wore a hat. His beautiful streaky
> golden hair streamed all over as the wind caught it. I was shocked by his
> freedom, but fascinated at the same time. He had lived all his life in France
> and he had a French accent and rolled his r's. He was like a wild creature.
> He never seemed to care what people thought. I felt when I walked down
> the street with him that he might suddenly fly away—he had so little
> connection with ordinary behavior.*

Laurence's accommodating bohemians eagerly accepted Peggy because she
gave such wonderful parties and because she was so starry-eyed about
Bohemia. Within a few months of their first meeting—the year was 1922—she
and Laurence were married, and following a long honeymoon in Italy, they
began a life of adventure and, sometimes, turmoil. Although for Peggy the
years ahead would be a period of self-indulgence, it was also a time when she
demonstrated her growing interest in and her great generosity to the artists and
writers who thronged around her and Laurence.

Most rich people are beset by those who want a share of their wealth, some
for very good and sound reasons, but there are also many who are simply
sponges on the well-to-do. Who is a real friend, and who is not? Who likes you
for your qualities and who flatters you for personal gain? A mistake of judgment sometimes leaves you with bitter memories. You become oversuspicious
of others without real cause. Whenever Peggy distributed any of her money,
she depended heavily on Laurence's advice, but even then neither could be
sure of another person's motives.

In such circumstances most people tend to build a protective wall around
themselves, usually by placing their money in a foundation whose adminis-
trators establish rules of judgment and turn away the unfit before they ever
reach the actual patron. It is safe, and it makes life less complicated. Peggy,
however, did not do this. She suffered through the demands of being a patron
largely alone, and it caused her much agony and grief. But from this ordeal
she gained. Little by little she acquired an intimate knowledge of the new art
of the twenties, particularly the work of the surrealists to whom Laurence was
allied and who were then just beginning to be recognized. Her sensitivity to
the qualities of art became stronger, her judgment more dependable.

Peggy also suffered from the people who avoided her simply because she
was wealthy, and there were many of them. They did not wish to be seen in her
company for fear they would be considered seekers of her generosity, and thus
she missed many who might have been her good friends. One, however, who
refused to allow wealth to stand in the way of friendship and who benefited
considerably from Peggy's assistance was the handsome Mina Loy. She was
the mother of two beautiful daughters, one of whom later married Julien Levy,

*Peggy Guggenheim. *Out of This Century*. (New York: Universe Books, 1979), pp. 23–24.

the New York art dealer who did so much to promote such painters as Salvador Dali, Max Ernst, and other surrealists in America. Mina was a poet of great talent as well as a painter. She was also an inventor and developed her own style of lampshades that looked like ships and cutout flowers which she framed in Louis Philippe frames she bought in the flea market. Laurence Vail christened them "Jade Blossoms." Peggy went all out to help Mina sell her lampshades in New York, where they had an immediate success. Alas, they were so successful that they were soon copied in wholesale quantities by local manufacturers. Nevertheless, Peggy did make a handsome profit for Mina while it lasted.

Laurence was such a gentlemen most of the time, such a fun-man, so sophisticated and worldly knowledgeable, that it was hard to believe that at other times, under the influence of drink, he could go completely haywire, causing horrendous scenes in public and engaging in pitched battles with those around him. These *bagarres* often led to police intervention, arrest, and sometimes brief stays in jail. The most famous of these squabbles took place in a Montparnasse café called Pirelli's, where the observant Jimmy Charters manned the bar. Here is what he told me about it.

Laurence, Peggy, and Laurence's ubiquitous sister, Clotilde, were having dinner on one side of the room, and five Frenchmen were having a boisterous meal on the other side. For unknown reasons, Laurence got the idea that the Frenchmen were making fun of his party, and without warning, he seized a bottle of vermouth and a bottle of Amer-Picon from the bar and hurled them in quick succession at the Frenchmen. The second bottle missed one of the diners by a fraction of an inch, leaving a big dent in the wall that for years afterward remained in evidence. Jimmy and the Frenchmen rushed Vail and beat him to the floor while the police, who arrived soon after, joined in the fracas. The police carried away what was left of Vail in a wheelbarrow, and he spent a couple of days in the local jail. The Frenchmen, or at least three of them, filed charges against Vail, and with good cause.

After Laurence had been removed, Peggy and Clotilde decided that the best thing they could do was to talk calmly and in a friendly fashion to the Frenchmen and ask them to consider withdrawing their complaints against Vail. Together they all sat down and two of the Frenchmen agreed to drop their charges, including the one who had escaped serious injury by such a small margin. The third, however, refused, and there matters stood. Two days later Peggy got her husband out of jail on bail, and when his trial came up two weeks later, she and her lawyer persuaded the judge to give him only a six-month suspended sentence. With that hanging over him, he was more careful where he threw bottles.

There was also a noteworthy by-product to this riotous evening. The man who had been nearly struck by Laurence's lethal bottle fell in love with Clotilde, a very romantic introduction indeed. They were married a few months later.

Peggy's marriage to Vail lasted seven years. They spent part of the time in

Peggy Guggenheim's friends Mina Loy (left) and Djuna Barnes *(Photo from the papers of Sylvia Beach, Princeton University Library).*

Montparnasse and part traveling in Italy, Austria, Switzerland, and Spain. There was even a memorable cruise on a barge up the Nile. Peggy bought a large house at Pramousquier, on the French Riviera. Mainly for summer use, it was a former hotel that contained plenty of rooms for their friends. There was no lack of them, despite the fact that the place lacked all the amenities her guests were used to having. Her life was one big party after another, interlarded with not infrequent public scenes with Laurence, though by and large they got on pretty well. She bore him two children, Sindbad in 1923 and Pegeen in 1925, both attractive youngsters. As time went on, she became more and more interested in helping promising writers and artists and in many cases gave them modest allowances so that they could pursue their work without gnawing financial need. She did this without ostentation, never telling the names of the recipients even in her uninhibited memoirs, *Out of This Century* (1946), based on a day-by-day diary she kept all through the years with meticulous care. The characters' names she changed and she thinly disguised them as parodies: Florenz Dale for her husband Laurence Vail, Ollie for his sister Clotilde, and Ray Soil for Kay Boyle, Vail's second wife. Even her own daughter's name was changed from Pegeen to Deirdre, while

Sindbad keeps his own name, as do many others—Marcel Duchamp for example, and Peggy's second husband Max Ernst.

But I am getting ahead of my story. After her separation and divorce from Vail, she met John Holms, an Englishman, a writer manqué, whose vast knowledge (he had an answer for every question) and affectionate attention provided just the stimulation and support she needed. For two years she and Holms did little but travel, sometimes with Pegeen (the court made Peggy the child's guardian), but never with Sindbad, who lived with his father. In 1934 Holms died, at only 37, and Peggy was again alone.

It was about this time that Peggy became more deeply interested in the surrealist movement. She thought she would like to be an art dealer and in that way promote knowledge and acceptance of this new art which many thought very strange indeed, even repulsive. With the help of Wyn Henderson, she set herself up in London, on Cork Street, where surrealism was almost unknown at that time and there put on one-man shows or group shows. Whatever she exhibited produced reams of newspaper and magazine publicity. She called her gallery Guggenheim Jeune in imitation of Bernheim Jeune in Paris, who had done so much to introduce impressionism to the world. Mary Reynolds and Marcel Duchamp were particularly helpful. At Duchamp's suggestion she opened her gallery with an exhibit of Jean Cocteau's work. She followed that success with exhibits of Tanguy, Arp, Kandinsky, Picasso, Brancusi, Braque, Masson, and Ernst. Unfortunately, the gallery did not make any money for its owner, but it did for the artists she exhibited. After a year and a half, however, she found that being an art dealer took too much time away from her parties and her private life. She decided to close the place—the year was 1939—and open a modern museum in or near London. It would be a more lasting venture and an easier one to manage. With the inestimable aid of the devoted Herbert Read (such "a distinguished-looking gentleman"), she started buying representative examples of modern art. Eventually she gave up her home in England, a lovely country house where Djuna Barnes, Peggy reported, wrote most of her best-known book, *Nightwood,* and went back to Paris and continued the systematic acquisition of a sizable collection of paintings and sculpture. It was Samuel Beckett, with whom she immediately fell in love, who now urged her to buy paintings by contemporary artists and even advised her which to purchase. With a burgeoning number of acquisitions, she looked in vain for a suitable building in which to house them and then gave up the search when it was apparent that a European war was in the making.

When the war finally came, she considered remaining in France, but later she decided that this was too dangerous, especially for her children. With the help of certain friends and her well provided checkbook, she collected her brood in Lisbon, where she waited for passage to New York on a Pan American Clipper.

It was really a family of sorts that she was taking back to the United States. First, there was her former husband, Laurence, and her future husband, the big, handsome, blond, and blue-eyed Max Ernst, whom she had again met in

Djuna Barnes, Paris, 1928 *(Photo courtesy of Miss Barnes).*

Paris shortly before the fall of the city. Then there was Laurence's second wife, Kay Boyle, from whom he was estranged and who lived in a separate hotel. Included, too, were Peggy's own children, Sindbad and Pegeen, now eighteen and sixteen, respectively, followed in age by Vail's three children by his second wife—Apple, eleven; Katie, seven; and Clover, two—and Kay Boyle's daughter by Ernest Walsh, Bobby, fourteen. In addition there was Jacqueline Ventadour, sixteen, the daughter of a close friend, Fanny, who had decided to sit it out in France, but wanted her daughter to attend school in America. Jacqueline, a lovely young girl, later married Sindbad, and after their divorce, she married the gifted French painter Jean Helion. Peggy, somewhat to her surprise, found herself the "mother" of this brood of ten.

She had appealed to the Louvre for room and permission to store her precious paintings there but was turned down because her collection was not considered worth saving. She managed, just two days before the Germans

Peggy Guggenheim at Art of This Century gallery before a painting by Pegeen, New York, 1940s *(Photo courtesy of Sindbad Vail).*

Peggy Guggenheim, 1978 *(Photo courtesy of Sindbad Vail).*

invaded Paris, to flee to Grenoble with all of her artworks, and from there to
Lisbon. After weeks of waiting, Peggy and her entourage finally took flight by
Clipper for New York, a far more comfortable way to cross the Atlantic than
the crowded sardine boxes in which we do it today, even though the elapsed
time of the trip was longer.

   In America, Peggy and Max Ernst married. Peggy opened another gallery,
Art of This Century, where she exhibited and promoted many American
abstract expressionist painters, notably Jackson Pollock, Robert Motherwell,
Mark Rothko, and Hans Hoffman. In 1947, longing to return to Europe, she
settled in a city she had always loved—Venice. Taking with her all her art but
not Max Ernst, whom she divorced before her departure, she established
herself in the handsome eighteenth-century Palazzo Venier dei Leoni on the
Grand Canal. Her collection at the time of her death in 1979 (she was eighty)
was estimated to be worth around thirty million dollars.

Gertrude Stein

IT was Hemingway, I think, who first took me in 1924 to the rue de Fleurus to meet Gertrude Stein. There she sat in her big chair in the center of her studio while the worshipers gathered around her, several of them seated on the huge cretonne sofa, listening closely so as not to lose a single pearl that might drop from her lips. Miss Stein was dressed in what appeared to be thick, heavy clothes, even in summer, ungainly, shapeless suits Hemingway called "steerage clothes." She dressed to play a part, to make herself a character, an eccentric. She and Alice B. Toklas (Gertrude's faithful companion and lover) wore leather sandals in the style of Raymond Duncan, and they may well have bought them from his craft shop on the rue Mazarine. Partly because of these plain clothes and partly because of her short, square stature, Gertrude looked like a peasant so often seen in the rural areas of many European countries. She had a large, flat head, its shape even more noticeable after she had had her hair cut short, which I could not but think was good for bottle dancing.*
Alice, thinner and slightly better dressed (she often wore straight dresses made of batiks), did not have this appearance, but she in turn was marked by a very pronounced hooked nose, black hair, gray eyes, and immaculately manicured nails. In her way she was as distinctive-looking as Gertrude.

At the rue de Fleurus I was introduced as a "young writer," but when Gertrude discovered that I was only a newspaperman who wrote occasional short pieces for magazines her interest waned. Just the same she put me through the rigid questionnaire that so many others had suffered and like most of them I was embarrassed and uncomfortable. Why this big lump of a woman, this Buddha in a corduroy uniform, should assume such an air of literary

*A South American dance requiring participants to balance a bottle on their heads while dancing.

Gertrude Stein, picnicking near Belley, 1926 *(Photo courtesy of Allen Tanner)*.

authority I could not understand. Nevertheless, I was a little awed by her, impressed in spite of myself.

"What do you write?" she asked.

"Words." I said.

"Don't be funny."

It was the wrong thing for me to have said. I should have replied that I was trying to find a rhythm of words and ideas as she herself had done so successfully. If I had kept my mouth shut, I would have been "an interesting young man with possibilities for the future." She would have offered to help me as she "had helped so many before." But I didn't say those things. I wasn't bright that way.

After a while she lost all interest in me and began to talk about herself. Her lips moved, her dark intelligent eyes, piercing yet kindly, moved, but the rest of her body was almost totally inert. All in her company were held by the depth of her eyes, which seemed to be looking at you in whatever part of the room you were standing, like the eyes of the horses in Rosa Bonheur's painting *The Horse Fair*. She often burst into hearty laughter, laughter like a beefsteak, Mable Dodge Luhan called it. She told us she was the greatest writer of her time, following the few masters who had preceded her such as Trollope and Henry James. She ignored writers in languages other than English since only English really counted. She pronounced all these "truths" with calm and firm assurance, as though they were established facts known to every, or at least almost every, schoolchild. No one laughed. For the moment, we all believed. Many of us continued to believe for a long time. Thus are myths created, thus does a person become a myth in his own time, thus does a worldwide reputation become established. This was a literary hoax of such a magnitude that it still has its believers today.

The only people that didn't believe were the publishers. Much to Gertrude's disgust, they stubbornly refused to print her books, but of course at that time they also refused to publish James Joyce, Ernest Hemingway, and a few others. Eventually, publishers made up for their lack of perception in regard to these new writers, but even today Gertrude Stein's works, while they may decorate the shelves of public libraries, are not extensively read.

Three Lives, a collection of three short stories she published at her own expense in 1909, is considered her best effort. But to appreciate *Three Lives*, or any of Miss Stein's books, one must have a particular feeling for the words and the rhythm of words, and one must not worry about any particular meaning the words may have. The critics largely ignored *Three Lives*, except for a few personal friends who reviewed it favorably out of freindship rather than literary conviction. Being ignored did not stop Gertrude, however. She went right on believing what Henry McBride told her, that she was an author who had a public but no publisher. In the 1920s she placed a few of her manuscripts with small presses, the most important being *The Making of Americans*, a swollen account of her ancestors that had been rejected by several publishers, which Robert McAlmon, after months of wearying negotiations with the demanding author, issued from his Contact Editions press. Finally, in 1930, fed up with uncooperative or unenlightened publishers, Gertrude and Alice founded their own press. Its purpose, Gertrude announced in plain English, was "to shove the unshoveable." They named it Plain Editions, and under its imprint they printed five of Gertrude's books in 1931 and 1932.

But the success of Gertrude's style, or at least the attention it attracted, was based largely on the desire of the intellectuals of that period—and even today—to find and admire all that was "new," meaning avant-garde. They operated on the premise that the more far-out a book was, the more important it must be, even if no one understood it. For the current crop of conservative college students it is an approach that has little appeal. Perhaps they agree with me that rhythms are good, but something else is needed to go with them, like meaning.

Just as important was the painstaking publicity that "La Stein" gave to her own writing, talking of her genius. She admitted that she was the only living literary genius, and she made no effort to conceal her scorn of other writers, notably James Joyce, whom she characterized as a pipsqueak, unworthy of even the slightest consideration.

Gertrude had a great magnetism, which drew her to many writers, such as Hemingway, Thornton Wilder, Carl Van Vechten, and Sherwood Anderson. Others, such as Ezra Pound, Robert McAlmon, and F. Scott Fitzgerald, were turned off by her self-praise and declarations of genius. McAlmon called her a mythomaniac and megalomaniac. For the curious hangers-on among us, she was an attraction like the bearded lady in the circus. Hosts of tourists flocked to get a glimpse of her, and if they succeeded, they felt their European trip

Gertrude Stein at her writing desk, rue de Fleurus, early 1920s *(Photo from the Collection of American Literature, Beinecke Rare Book and Manuscript Library, Yale University).*

had been worthwhile. Gertrude loved this curiosity and adoration. Sylvia Beach used to take whole parties of tourists over to see Gertrude Stein by prearrangement with the tenets of the rue de Fleurus. As the tourists spread the word, so her reputation and fame gathered momentum.

Many of the guests came for the cakes and cookies prepared by Alice, for they were always excellent and satisfying to the hungry bohemians, though the liquid refreshments, except for tea, flowed less generously. Still, as free lunches went, it was pretty good and worth spending an hour listening to the literary exploits and aspirations of Gertrude.

I only went three times to Gertrude's salon, for I found it a bore once the novelty had worn off. She said the same things over and over again because the spectators, the guests if you like, tended to change with each new session. Of course there were the little dinners for eight or ten at which favorites were entertained and the conversations no doubt varied, but I never rose to that rank. Hemingway said they were a bore, and I believed him. Pound, like me, never returned to the rue de Fleurus after his first couple of visits. He was hardly the sort to worship at anyone's shrine.

Gertrude Stein and her brother Leo had come to Europe from San Francisco in 1900, and Gertrude had first established herself in London. Leo divided his time between Italy and Paris. He finally settled down in Paris at 27 rue de Fleurus and was joined there by his sister in 1904.

Leo was an artist but was more skilled as an art critic and philosopher. He had become acquainted with the Paris art world well before Gertrude arrived. It was he who "discovered" Picasso, Matisse, Braque, and others of that era. Leo would not have liked me to use the word "discovered" in regard to his appreciation of their painting. He merely recognized their worth and showed it most wisely by buying their canvases. When Gertrude arrived on the scene, she too appreciated the works of these painters, in part at least because she tended to follow at that early stage all the leads of her older brother. Her late claim that she had "discovered" Picasso and others was not well founded. I think it is safe to say that it was Leo alone who had the taste to recognize the artistic talent of these painters who were later to be recognized so widely, although it was Gertrude who made personal friendships with them, encouraged them to visit the Stein establishment, and often entertained them. They appreciated her as a friend and a companion in the avant garde movement in art and literature that was slowly growing in Europe and America.

Although Gertrude went along with Leo in his choice of painters, she does not seem to have had any real artistic flair. Mabel Dodge Luhan was probably right when she said that Gertrude didn't care what was considered good taste. If something, including paintings, "affected her pleasantly" she enjoyed it and perhaps obtained it for that reason. Later, when she no longer had Leo's judgment to lean on, she made some astonishingly bad choices in artists to praise and collect, notably Sir Francis Rose, whose popular portraits were as banal as one could find. Nevertheless, Leo and Gertrude seemed to live in harmony until Alice came along.

I was personally very fond of Leo, with whom I used to drink and talk for hours on the terrace of the Dôme or the Closerie des Lilas. Handicapped by deafness, Leo had a hearing aid, but he did not like to wear it, and when he was without it you had to shout to make yourself heard. He also shouted, assuming that everyone else was deaf, too. The result was, of course, that I did more listening than talking. Leo was a keen-minded romantic, a warm personality who attracted many women. He was not a doer, but a delightful dreamer with a fine intellectual background. We both attended the Academie Julien. I do not now remember just what we talked about. It must have been art, principally, I think, and the things he had seen and the people of Europe, particularly the French. Unlike Gertrude, he had a good knowledge of French and a rapport with the people. For me, just out of college, he was very stimulating.

Leo and Gertrude developed some basic differences of opinion, and these led eventually to the break between them. In the first place, Leo did not approve of Picasso's espousal of the cubist style and thought that he had forsaken his true calling in the postimpressionist world. Leo thought Picasso's work was that of a great genius up to the time when the artist embraced cubism. After that, Leo regarded him as a skilled and clever painter but as one perverted in his concept of painting. Gertrude sided with Picasso.

There was worse to come. Leo did not feel that Gertrude's writing had true literary validity. Picasso thought it was part of the new movement in art, such as the entrance of cubism in painting. "What she writes," Leo told me later, "is sheer nonsense." He found no merit in such examples of the "pure" Stein as this:

A COMPLETED PORTRAIT OF PICASSO

If I told him would he like it. Would he like it if I told him.

Would he like it would Napoleon would Napoleon would would he like it.

If Napoleon if I told him if I told him if Napoleon. Would he like it if I told him if I told him if Napoleon. Would he like it if Napoleon if Napoleon if I told him. If I told him if Napoleon if Napoleon if I told him. If I told him would he like it would he like it if I told him.

Shutters shut and open so do queens. Shutters shut and shutters and so shutters shut and shutters and so and so shutters and so shutters shut and shutters and so. And so shutters shut and so and also. And also and so and so and so and also. Let me recite what History teaches, History teaches.*

On the other hand, there was the "impure" Stein, which had a popular success. It began with Gertrude's desire to see a book published about the Gertrude Stein myth and so she sat down to ghost it for Alice B. Toklas, using the language that she thought Alice would use. The public was dying for a simple uncomplicated explanation of what Stein was all about, and they got it in *The Autobiography of Alice B. Toklas,* a best-seller from the day it was published. It is the only book of Stein's which had any success.

Gertrude was deeply hurt by Leo's desertion. She felt betrayed by the one person with whom she had had the closest personal and intellectual rapport. In 1913, Leo moved out of the rue de Fleurus, never to return, never to settle his quarrel with his sister. He continued to live in Paris, however, and to circulate in artistic circles, to paint and to write. He was noted for his eloquent letters.

Gertrude's life had been profoundly changed in 1907 by her meeting with Alice Bessie Toklas, a thirty-year-old young woman from San Francisco, who

*Gertrude Stein. *Portraits and Prayers*. (New York: Random House, 1934), p. 68.

Gertrude Stein reading in her studio, rue de Fleurus, early 1920s *(Photo from the Collection of American Literature, Beinecke Rare Book and Manuscript Library, Yale University).*

had come to Paris for the usual European jaunt with Harriet Levy, a friend also from San Francisco. Alice had known Michael Stein through Harriet when he and his wife Sara lived in San Francisco. He was Gertrude's much older brother, and when Alice arrived and found that they were also in Paris, she looked them up at once. Michael and Sara were buying paintings and conducting a salon much along the lines of Gertrude's. Through Michael, Alice soon met Gertrude.

It was certainly love at first sight. Both had had lesbian liaisons before, and they knew and accepted the true nature of this kind of love without hesitation, doubt, or reluctance. It was a long time before they acknowledged their love to each other, however, and an even longer time before Alice moved into the apartment on the rue de Fleurus. But almost from the very beginning, Alice spent most of her time there, typing Gertrude's manuscripts every morning and in the afternoons and evenings helping with the entertaining of visitors, or taking long walks around Paris with her, and sometimes going on trips into the country, to Bellay and later Bilignin, for days or weeks at a time. Finally, in September 1910, after Leo had moved away and Harriet had decided that she would definitely return to San Francisco, Alice began to share the apartment and join her life completely with that of Gertrude. For the next thirty-three years they were never separated, sharing an attachment which ripened into a husband-wife relationship to endure for the rest of their lives, "until death do us part."

There is no need to point out, I suppose, that in this congenial marriage Alice's role as the wife included that of a housekeeper, cook, typist, gardener, travel agent, bookkeeper, and entertainer of the dull wives that sometimes accompanied the interesting guests at the rue de Fleurus and later at the rue Christine. She pursued these household administrative and social duties with assiduous care and devotion and with an extraordinary social virtuosity, and one must assume that she played the more personal role of confidant and close companion with the same ardor.

Of course Alice's attachment to Gertrude played a part in Leo's break with his sister, although this was not mentioned at the time. Alice says in her memoirs that Leo behaved badly, but refrained from further explanation or comment. Leo did not accept the position of an also-ran. He knew that he had been largely the person who found Picasso, Matisse, and Juan Gris and that it was he who urged Gertrude to buy their works while they were still unknowns. They had bought these pictures together, and Leo had a half interest in the collection. Also, one must presume that when Alice came to make a ménage à trois, she brought certain problems with her. One had the feeling that Leo's departure did not seem a great loss to Gertrude and that to Alice it must have been a relief. Alice, seemingly so meek and mild, so self-effacing in outward appearance, had strong possessive feelings locked up within her heart. Anyone to whom Gertrude showed too much attachment must somehow be eliminated. When Hemingway and Gertrude became too chummy, too interested in each other's work and concepts, Alice moved skillfully, catlike, to separate them. Alice won. Alice always won. On another occasion, Gertrude and Alice visited a friend of Gertrude's, Mable Dodge (later Mabel Dodge Luhan) at the Fiesoli. Mabel, a benefactor who helped to publish Gertrude's works, seemed to have a particular liking for Gertrude and Gertrude also for her, but once again Alice intervened and once again retained her partner. Doubtless Gertrude would have done likewise had Alice shown a special interest in another, but Alice, the faithful and the possessive, never made such a mistake.

More and more Alice took over the reins in their way of life. It was Alice who managed the household, worried about income, and entertained the wives so that Gertrude could concentrate on the men. Her primary concern, however, was to induce publishers to print some of Gertrude's many, many manuscripts.

When World War I came, Alice and Gertrude decided to remain in France, and after awhile they began distributing supplies for the relief of civil populations. Gertrude used a Ford (christened Godiva), which she had purchased at her own expense, for this work, and Alice sat beside her, taking care of the accounts, as they drove from one end of France to the other. It was a good effort, though not as heroic as some have portrayed it. It was definitely a worthwhile contribution to the war effort.

Gertrude Stein and Pavel Tchelitchev, Russian painter, seated in "Godiva," near Belley, 1926 *(Photo courtesy of Allen Tanner).*

Gertrude Stein writing in her studio, rue de Fleurus, early 1920s *(Photo from the Collection of American Literature, Beinecke Rare Book and Manuscript Library, Yale University).*

When the war ended, they returned to the rue de Fleurus, the Saturday gatherings, the constant entertainment of those Gertrude had chosen as the young men of promise, such as Pavel Tchelitchev, Allen Tanner, Virgil Thomson, Bravig Imbs, and Georges Hugnet, on all of whom she had bestowed a special Stein blessing. It should be noted that there were no young women in this group, only men.

Hemingway was, I think, flattered by the attention he received from Gertrude, although he never admitted it to me. On the other hand, he spoke quite violently against her in some conversations we had in 1933 when he wrote the introduction to the book I ghosted for James Charters (Jimmy the Barman). The introduction was an attack on Gertrude Stein, though he did not name her by name. It is quite evident that the woman in question could only be Gertrude. In talking to me about it at the time, he promised that some day when he wrote his own memoirs of Montparnasse, presumably in what was to be called *A Moveable Feast,* he would really get her. He thought that the introduction to my book was not strong enough, and he offered to do it over again, but since he was leaving for Africa in a few days, I was afraid that if he took it away, I would wind up without any introduction at all. He was at that time living in a small Paris hotel with his second wife Pauline and two sons and being very secretive about his goings and comings, swearing the few of us who saw him to the utmost secrecy. This was a foretaste of the paranoia which would eventually lead to his suicide in Idaho in 1961. Hemingway again mentioned his determination to "get even" with Gertrude when he wrote his book on the characters on Montparnasse. He was particularly infuriated by her claim that she had "discovered" him and had helped him find a publisher. "It is we who tried like hell to find a publisher for *her.*"

Hemingway told me on more than one occasion that he derived nothing from Gertrude, that is, no literary stimulus, yet he seems to have told others that he did indeed learn about the rhythm of words and the use of repetition from her writing.

Hemingway's attack on Gertrude in the introduction to my book was followed by a more angry lambasting which he gave her in his next book, *The Green Hills of Africa,* which he wrote in 1933 and 1934. But again he did not mention her by name. In *A Moveable Feast,* he devoted two early chapters to her and treated her very gently and warmly indeed. The old animosity seemed to have vanished. In a later chapter called "A Strange Enough Ending," however, Hemingway describes the end of their relationship in a scene set early in their friendship that must be called malicious. Waiting at the rue de Fleurus apartment for Gertrude and Alice to come downstairs, Hemingway overheard the two women quarreling. Alice spoke to Gertrude in a way he "had never heard one person speak to another." Gertrude, he then heard, pleaded with Alice. "Don't pussy. Don't. Don't, please don't. I'll do anything, pussy, please don't do it." Hemingway left without seeing either woman. What he had heard might have been a confirmation for him of their lesbianism, and his account clearly suggests that Alice's powerful dominance over Gertrude came as a shock. But I find it hard to believe that he turned against her because he discovered that she and Alice were lesbians and that his alleged horror of homosexuality drove out all the admiration he had had for her previously. That Gertrude and Alice were attached by something more than just girlish friendship was apparent to everyone in Montparnasse, and Hemingway must have known it. I do not remember that he ever mentioned it to me, but there was not any reason why he should comment on such an obvious fact.

In 1934, the great success of *The Autobiography of Alice B. Toklas* preceding them, Gertrude and Alice returned to the United States for the first time since they had left so that Gertrude could lecture on her writings at various universities. Her reception in America was mixed. Crowds came to meet her and to hear her talk about her writing, but the students were for the most part skeptical of its value. Some, however, were impressed by anything new, and her writing was really avant-garde. At home Gertrude was as opinionated as she was in Paris. "Sweet Briar and Mt. Holyoke," she proclaimed, "are the only two colleges where the girls are not typed. Those at Smith, Vassar, and Wellesley will always be Smith, Vassar, and Wellesley." Among the many who entertained the traveling ladies were Thornton Wilder and Carl Van Vechten.

Gertrude Stein and Alice B. Toklas with Carl Van Vechten during the author's lecture tour of the United States, 1943 (*Photo from the Collection of American Literature, Beinecke Rare Book and Manuscript Library, Yale University*).

In 1938 Gertrude and Alice vacated the rue de Fleurus apartment when the owner decided to give it to his son for a wedding present. To their new quarters at 5 rue Christine, they moved 130 canvases. As World War II approached, their visitors slowly diminished, and when war came, they along with the other Americans were urged to leave France and return to the United States. Both Gertrude and Alice felt that their attachment to the country in which they had already spent so many years was stronger than any desire for safety. They also felt that no one would bother two old women even if their nationality was suspect. When France fell and the Germans occupied most of the country and particularly when the United States declared war, they were again urged to leave, and again they resisted the pleas of their friends. A certain number of other Americans who had remained in France were confined to camps by the Germans, but were not on the whole treated badly. No one paid any attention to Gertrude and Alice who were living quietly in their rented cottage at Bilignin in Burgundy wine country.

Both food and other supplies were scarce, and Gertrude could no longer indulge in the fine culinary delights of which she was so fond. To make up for this loss, Alice invented a fanciful substitute. For years Gertrude had been in the habit of giving Alice a handsome new cookbook as a Christmas present, and now Alice started reading from these books every evening, producing dreams of luscious dishes one by one instead of the real thing. This seemed to satisfy them both, and Gertrude lost considerable weight as a result. In the middle of the war the landlord asked to have his house back. The women moved to Culoz nearby where they continued their life in the same manner, except that there was no large garden for Alice's pleasure. Here, however, they came in contact with the war for the first time when German and later Italian soldiers were quartered in their house, but they encountered no hardships and, in fact, found the Italians very *sympathique*.

At one point they became seriously short of money and were forced to sell a Cézanne portrait of his wife which they had brought with them from Paris. To do this they had to carry it to the Swiss border and across without attracting attention. This they managed without incident, returning to France just as quietly with the money they had obtained, a considerable sum.

Then, in August 1944, two American war correspondents appeared in the doorway of their cottage, Eric Sevareid and the late Frank Gervasi, declaring they were there to liberate these two famous women and their white poodle "Basket II" and to inform their many friends at home that they were safe and well.

After the war, Gertrude and Alice returned to Paris where the rue Christine apartment once more became a collecting point for their many literary and artistic friends. It was exhilarating to be living again in the city Gertrude called her "hometown," even if the long occupation had made it rather drab. When they felt the urge for a change, they still traveled to the nearby countryside or as far as Bilignin. Such excursions from Paris were not so easily accomplished as they had once been, however. For one thing, Gertrude's

Alice B. Toklas (seated) with Thornton Wilder, Morrill Cody, and Man Ray, at exhibit "American Writers in Paris and Their Friends," Paris, 1959 (*Photo from the collection of Morrill Cody*).

health had weakened. Headed south on one such trip, taken so that Gertrude could rest after feeling fatigued, she felt especially ill at Azay le Rideaw, where a local physician sent them back to Paris. A nephew of Gertrude's had an ambulance take her, Alice by her side, to the American hospital in Neuilly. She was operated on and found to have cancer of the intestines. The doctors said that she had apparently had it for years. Gertrude Stein died on the evening of July 27, 1946.

And so began Alice's long widowhood. Twenty years of solitude and suffering, both mental and physical, waiting for the day when she could join her Gertrude in heaven. Her memory of Gertrude never dimmed. If anything, her attachment became ever more intense. She identified herself ever more closely with her companion of so many years. She spoke of herself in the plural as though Gertrude were still there, and she defended her writing against any criticism, even mere analysis by outsiders. If Gertrude's work was attacked in print or in personal letters, Alice would rush to her defense with uncommon severity. More and more she lived in a closed world, rarely visited by friends. Although she did not become embittered, she kept more and more to herself, seeing only a few old friends or outsiders, if they were properly introduced.

Alice took an active interest in the big retrospective exposition of the American writers of the twenties and their French and British friends which I directed in Paris in 1959. She contributed materials to the considerable section on Gertrude Stein, and under the aegis of Thornton Wilder, she spent several hours at the opening sitting at one of the old café tables we had assembled for the occasion. There she "received" in much the same way that Gertrude had greeted her guests at the rue de Fleurus. Alice was, for the occasion, the strongest symbol and representative of the literary and artistic glories of times past. She was by far the oldest person present. She was also noted for her "mustache." It became another personal symbol. She was proud of it and resisted any idea of having it removed. People admired Alice and the "beauty" of her mustache.

Nancy Cunard

I don't remember just when or where I first saw Nancy Cunard, although it must have been in the early twenties and certainly in Montparnasse, but I do have a vivid recollection of what she looked like. Stunning, I suppose, is the word most often used to describe her appearance. Tall and slender to the point of frailty, Nancy carried herself with an erect military bearing. She walked quickly and with an unusual scissorslike movement of her long legs. She always seemed to be leading others, always out in front a step or two. Her posture and that perceptible determination in her gait created the impression that here was a person capable of great action. Her small but well shaped head had a sculptured look, and her features, sharply defined and almost metallically white, were accented by a pair of light blue eyes rimmed with kohl. No one ever forgot Nancy's eyes. She could bring them to a sharp point and penetrate one's strongest defenses. Her tawny blonde hair was as short as Duff Twysden's, but Nancy provided an added delight—two tight ringlets that dangled along each temple. She named them "my beavers," and they remained one of the two badges she retained for the rest of her life. The other was her ivory bracelets.

Nancy began collecting ivory soon after she arrived in Paris in 1920. Within a few years she had accumulated over four hundred pieces. Among the first people she knew in Paris were the then very active surrealists André Breton, Paul Eluard, and a third, Louis Aragon, who fell desperately in love with her. Nancy absorbed their enthusiasm for African and Oceanic art, and since she had the means to satisfy this taste, she and Aragon haunted French and English seaports in search of ivories that returning sailors sold to local shopkeepers. That these treasure hunts were successful was a well-known fact in Montparnasse, for it was Nancy's habit to appear in our crowded cafés with her long, thin arms encased from wrist to elbow in ivory bracelets. They formed what one might call ivory sleeves. It is hardly a violation of truth to say that one could hear Nancy before one saw her. Hearing her bracelets was like suddenly harkening to an approaching locomotive still too far off to see or hidden by some obstruction. In addition to whatever auditory and visual delight Nancy and her admirers may have derived from the sight and sound of clinking ivories, they occasionally stood the wearer in good stead as convenient and effective weapons. The sight of one of Nancy's spurned lovers nursing painful head wounds was awesome proof of their efficacy and their owner's skill.

Oil portrait of Nancy Cunard attired in her father's Ascot outfit, by Eugene MacCown, American artist and sometime companion of Miss Cunard, Paris, 1923 (Photo from the collection of Hugh Ford).

Nancy Cunard wearing a feathered headpiece and gazing into a "crystal ball," late 1920s (Photo courtesy of Mrs. Curtis Moffit).

Nancy was part American. Her mother, born Maud Burke in San Francisco in 1872, first penetrated the secure bastion of the English aristocracy in 1895, when she married the grandson of the founder of the Cunard Steamship Line, Sir Bache Cunard. Maud was twenty-three, her husband forty-three. A year later their only child, Nancy Clara, was born, and Maud happily followed custom and relinquished the infant to the first of a series of nurses and governesses who raised and educated her. By then Sir Bache and his wife had decided to follow separate paths. Sir Bache, preferring seclusion, toiled at his hobby of metal work and ran with his hounds. Maud turned her gaze to London and the bright social events that remained beyond her grasp. It was to a rambling, Georgian edifice in Leicestershire called Nevill Holt, a day's journey from London, that Sir Bache had brought his young bride. And it was there that he hoped they would live a quiet country life. But for Maud the bucolic pleasures of rural England paled next to the enticements of the fashionable world she craved. If the wife of Sir Bache was to be denied the society of that world, she would retaliate by inviting the denizens of that world to the country. Maud's weekend parties at Nevill Holt bored Sir Bache, but they furnished all the excitement and companionship his wife desired. They also strengthened her resolve to hasten her departure for London.

Until she married in 1916, Nancy lived with her parents (after 1911 with her mother), seeing mainly her governesses, her male cousins, and her mother's elegant admirer, the Irish writer George Moore. The friendship that developed between the author of fifty years and Nancy became the strongest of her early life. He was, she wrote later, my "first friend." During his extended visits at Nevill Holt, Moore would often take Nancy for long walks in the countryside. Along the way, he would identify the trees and the flowers and recite his poetry and supply his young companion with the names of the world's greatest poets. Not many years later when Nancy began writing her own poetry, it was to her "first friend" that she turned for guidance.

In 1911, Maud abandoned both Nevill Holt and Sir Bache for London. By now her name had become romantically linked with Sir Thomas Beecham as well as Moore, who also relocated in London the same year. She took a house in Cavendish Square and set out to realize her ambition to be a hostess at least as grand as Margot Asquith or the duchess of Rutland. She let it be known that henceforth she preferred to be called "Emerald" rather than Maud. Nancy accompanied her mother.

Emerald's removal to London and her triumph as a leading society figure produced the first serious strains between mother and daughter that would eventually culminate in estrangement. Nancy objected to the restrictions imposed upon the members of the circles Emerald inhabited. When Emerald insisted on "bringing out" her daughter, a bored and defiant Nancy truculently attended the debutante balls given in her honor, and even agreed to be presented at court. But unknown to her mother, she was making her own friends—a "Corrupt Coterie," she called them—among whom were the poets and painters Osbert Sitwell, Evan Morgan, Iris Tree, Alvaro "Chile" Guevara,

Robert Nichols, and Augustus John. Their heated talk of poetry, painting, jazz, and liberal politics provided all the substance and wit absent from Emerald's conventional world. Or so Nancy believed. When she announced her engagement to a young Australian, who had been wounded at Gallipoli, named Sydney Fairbairn, Emerald was thunderstruck. "Are you sure you want to go through with it?" she queried. "I gave my word and I must," Nancy replied. They married in November 1916. Both were twenty. Marriage accomplished what Nancy wanted—freedom from Emerald and a chance to live her own life. Otherwise, it was a disappointment. Sydney lacked all that she so much admired in the members of the "Corrupt Coterie." It was a relief when, recovered from his wounds, he joined the Grenadier Guards and left for France. A year later they separated, and Nancy, refusing to live with Emerald again, took a small house with a friend. She remarked later that her marriage had been "a detestable period, a caesura between many good things past and further good things to come." Chief among the "good things" ahead was moving to Paris in January 1920.

Paris, besides serving as an escape from her mother's influence (what little remained of it) and appealing to her rebelliousness, nurtured her burgeoning artistic interests, especially poetry. Her first collection, *Outlaws*, appeared the year after she arrived; a second and larger one, *Sublunary*, followed in 1923; and *Parallax*, which Virginia and Leonard Woolf printed at their Hogarth Press, came in 1925. Ironically, however, her poetry attracted less attention at the time than the art she inspired among artists and writers.

Constantin Brancusi sculpted her in wood; Man Ray, Curtis Moffat, and Cecil Beaton photographed her; and for painters such as Alvaro Guevara, Oskar Kokoschka, and Eugene MacCown she sat for portraits. But it was rather as a character model for several writers that Nancy won immense popularity and permanent fame. After using Nancy and Emerald as the "originals" of his heroine and her mother in his first novel, *Piracy*, Michael Arlen wrote a best-seller called *The Green Hat*, in which the "real" heroine, a charismatic beauty named Iris March, could only have been inspired by Nancy Cunard. In 1928, she made another fictional appearance as Lucy Tantamount in Aldous Huxley's novel *Point Counter Point*. Huxley, like Arlen, Guevara, Robert Nichols, and Wyndham Lewis, had been infatuated with Nancy a few years earlier. His "portrait" of that affair, with its fitful seizures of passion and its agonizing collapse, reveals a Nancy whose "masculine detachment" allows her to break with her lovers with impunity. A few people have argued that because Lady Brett Ashley in *The Sun Also Rises* also indulged herself sexually without much discretion or feeling and because she was well connected, strong willed, and dissolute, Hemingway must have modeled her on Nancy. But this is untrue. Hemingway scarcely knew Nancy, and only Duff Twysden among the author's acquaintances could have been the actual counterpart of Lady Brett.

While hardly a femme fatale, Nancy did have a reputation for attracting men, many men, and then bringing them to their knees before she discarded

Wood sculpture *Jeune Fille Sophistiquée* (Sophisticated Young Girl, N.C.) by Constantin Brancusi, Paris, 1925 *(Photograph by Duane Michals).*

Nancy Cunard, **oil painting, by John Banting, English artist and longtime friend, 1930 *(Photo from the collection of Hugh Ford).***

them. There were exceptions, of course. Her one-year liaison with Ezra Pound probably caused Nancy more torment than Pound. But this was not true of the longer and much more intimate relationship with Louis Aragon, from which Aragon emerged with deeper wounds than Nancy. Many common interests, with writing the most binding, held them together. They were ideal companions, and a more striking couple few had ever before seen. They could even labor side by side. In 1928, when Nancy announced she would open a little press and print books by hand, Aragon joined in enthusiastically. Whatever misgivings he had about the feasibility of the project he kept to himself. To many of us it seemed inconceivable that this highborn renegade-socialite could be serious. While Montparnassians waited to see what would happen, Nancy went to see two fledgling printers, Virginia and Leonard Woolf, who, while not intentionally dissuasive, let go an anguished warning that Nancy promptly forgot. "My dear," they chorused, "your hands will always be covered with ink!" Others echoed the Woolfs' cry, with no more success, for Nancy, as always, made her own path.

As far as I know, Nancy's is the only press that holds the distinction of having been born in a stable. It was one of the outbuildings that came with a Norman farmhouse Nancy purchased near Vernon in 1927, so that she could live and love and print books in privacy. The press she christened the Hours, a name at once dullish, but suitable, and appropriately suggestive of work. Where the stanchions had been, Nancy installed an immense Mathieu press, at least a century old, on which a friend named Bill Bird had recently hand-printed Hemingway's book *In Our Time*. Bird also supplied an experienced instructor who had once worked as a printer's devil and who, to his alarm, soon found this amateur annoyingly unimpressionable and as unconventional as the books she intended to publish. Efforts to instruct his charge, as well as Aragon, in the intricacies of the Black Art failed dismally. She would learn from him, Nancy announced, quickly, all she possibly could. Meanwhile, she would put innovation and experimentation ahead of his timeworn practices. No one, wrote Nancy later, ever launched out on a new endeavor so sailless, mastless, provisionless, uncompassed, and abashed.

That Nancy had realized a few of her goals after a year was miraculous. Of the announced volumes of modern poetry, those by Iris Tree and Pound had not appeared, but others by Alvaro Guevara and Aragon had. So had the prose pieces of Norman Douglas, Richard Aldington, and George Moore. She had produced eight books, all hand-printed. Her success she attributed to hard work, a few celebrated authors, almost total ignorance of the customs and practices of printing, and good luck.

Of the twenty-four Hours books Nancy published, sixteen lay ahead at the start of 1930. They would consist of collections of poetry by Roy Campbell, Laura Riding, Walter Lowenfels, Ezra Pound, and Robert Graves; a catalogue for an exhibit of paintings by the American Eugene MacCown; prose by Aldington, Havelock Ellis, and George Moore; and two books which would become memorials to her inspiration and ingenuity—one, a mosaic of the arts titled *Henry-Music*, combined poetry, impeccable printing, photomontage, and music; the other, as the reader will soon see, would have to be called a literary discovery.

In 1930, Nancy left the quiet Norman countryside and moved back to Paris. In her new location in the rue Guenégaud, near the river, she announced the Hours Press would hold a poetry contest. A prize of ten pounds would be awarded for the best poem on the subject of time. The announcement released an avalanche of verse. In a few weeks, over a hundred specimens descended on the Hours Press shop, ranging from doggerel to a kind of sham metaphysics. From the accumulation Nancy and Richard Aldington (her co-judge) sifted through the entries that might charitably qualify for the award, and then stoically resigned themselves to giving the prize to the best of the mediocre entries, unless by some miracle a truly first-rate poem turned up before the closing date. None did. The deadline arrived and passed. But unknown to them, a winning poem was in the making, and it was Nancy who discovered it the morning after the contest closed when she opened the shop and spied tucked beneath the door a small folder bearing the strange word *Whoroscope*, under which was the signature, Samuel Beckett. The name meant nothing to her, nothing to Aldington, but the poem inside filled them with admiration. "What remarkable lines, what images and analogies, what vivid coloring; indeed, what technique." Beckett was summoned to the rue Guenégaud and told that he had won the competition; and he, in turn, told the astonished judges that he had only learned of the contest the previous day and had composed the entire poem of ninety-eight lines in two frenzied stints separated by a refreshing interlude at the Cochon de Lait for a guzzle of salad and Chambertin, after which, near dawn, he had delivered it to her door. *Whoroscope*, suited in red covers and adorned with a white sash that bore the proud notice it was the prizewinner, soon appeared and was prominently placed in Nancy's display window. It was Beckett's first separately published work.

The man who replaced Louis Aragon in Nancy's life and who became the only man she ever truly loved and who transformed her into a dedicated and impassioned crusader was a black jazz pianist from Washington, D.C., named Henry Crowder. Nancy had found him playing in a Venice nightclub with a quartet called Eddie South and His Alabamians. Captivated by the music but more by the black man's physical appearance, she persuaded him to leave the group and become her assistant at the press. Crowder agreed, and for the next four years he accompanied Nancy on two continents, across the Atlantic, to every region of France, and on visits to London that infuriated Emerald and led to the final break between Nancy and her mother. There were times when Henry wished he had never met Nancy Cunard, times when he was made to feel he was just another of Nancy's casual lovers and could be dropped at any moment. But he hung on, and so did Nancy. Each introduced the other to new and exotic worlds. Nancy's aristocratic friends and her upbringing amazed Crowder, but even more astonishing was Henry's description of the black man's existence in America. As she listened to him tell of his poor childhood in Georgia and the life he had eked out later in Washington as a piano player in a brothel, her reactions changed from disbelief, to absorption, to anger, to outrage. His charge that his own country could be the worst place on earth for a black man was something that needed to be documented.

Nancy's personal investigation into the relations between the black and white races began in 1931; it ended in 1934 with the publication of a monumental anthology called *Negro*. For more than two years and at great expense, Nancy collected materials for her book in England, Europe, and the United States. From friends like William Carlos Williams, Ezra Pound, and George Antheil and from dozens of new acquaintances like Langston Hughes, George Padmore, Sterling Brown, Jomo Kenyatta, and Sylvia Townsend Warner, she received hundreds of contributions. She dedicated *Negro* to Henry Crowder.

Nancy examined black life not just in the United States, but in the West Indies, Africa, South America, and Europe as well. She investigated all aspects of black culture—entertainment, literature, art, and music. She wanted to prove "that there was no superior race, merely cultural differences, that racism [had] no basis whatsoever." Unfortunately, her romantic attraction to communism and a belief that it alone could solve the problems blacks faced vitiated the overall impact of her work, but despite the presence of too much communist dogmatism, the anthology was an ambitious and historic document that brought blacks and whites together fifty years ago in a common effort to present a problem that remains unsolved.

Once stirred, Nancy's sense of injustice never diminished. After a trip to Russia in August 1935, where her American friends Langston Hughes and William Patterson assured her (wrongly, as it turned out) that *Negro* would be translated into Russian, she traveled to Geneva to report the League of Nations debates on the Ethiopian crisis. Her dispatches to the Associated Negro Press (U.S.) revealed a supreme disgust with the "suprahuman cynicism" that motivated the actions of the large powers. She vowed to tell the truth in her own book, *Ethiopia Betrayed—Imperialism. How Long?*, which she began at once. But when civil war broke out in Spain, she persuaded a friend to finish it for her.

Nancy's participation in the Spanish war lasted until the final, dreary months of the struggle. From the time she first went to Spain in August 1936, a month after the conflict began, until the fighting ended in the spring of 1939, she made four trips to the country. A passionate antifascist, she added her voice to a chorus of left-wing invective against the usurper Franco and his supporters Hitler and Mussolini. In 1937, she polled British writers on their attitudes toward the war in Spain and published their predominately pro-Loyalist statements in a booklet called *Authors Take Sides on the Spanish Civil War*. She also printed seveal plaquettes of war poetry, one of which was W. H. Auden's first version of his poem "Spain." Nancy's last effort on behalf of Republican Spain was assisting refugees interned in camps near the Franco-Spanish border, several of whom, including the poet Cesar Arconada, stayed in her Normandy farmhouse until they resettled.

Returning to her beloved France after the Second World War, which she had passed in London working for the Free French, was a bittersweet experience. Sadly she saw that what she had learned from friends in France about the destruction of her home in Normandy was true. A near ruin, it was uninhabitable, but even if she were to rebuild it, she doubted if she would ever want to live in the region again. Lost or mutilated in two separate sackings, one by German soldiers, the other by French peasants, were her paintings, drawings, African figures, manuscripts, books, and letters. In central France, near the hamlet of Lamothe-Fénélon, in Lot, not so very far from the chateau Josephine Baker inhabited with her "rainbow" family, Nancy found a new home, another ancient farmhouse. She named it Peyrouro. There she lived, often alone, for the last twenty years of her life. In the early fifties,

Nancy Cunard displays a few ivory bracelets, La Monthe-Fenelon (Lot), France, 1963 (*Photo from the collection of Hugh Ford*).

she began setting down memories of Norman Douglas, perhaps occasioned by his death in 1952, and in 1954 they appeared under the title *Grand Man: Memories of Norman Douglas*. Two years later, she completed a similar book about another old friend, George Moore. Her last publication, done with the assistance of Hugh Ford, was an informal history of her Hours Press, *These Were the Hours*. Always opposed to books that romanticized the period in Paris between the wars, she made sure that the account avoided gossip and sometimes even literary anecdotes. Too ill in the final years of her life to remain alone in the farmhouse except during summers, Nancy would reside in a hotel in Toulouse from September until June or July. When that became too great an effort for her, she lived with friends on the Riviera. She was often depressed, lonely, quarrelsome, and restless. Her main comfort came from composing a long poem about "visions" experienced by the bards of the Middle Ages, on which she was working when, following an argument with her friends, she suddenly entrained for Paris, where, on March 17, 1965, six days after her sixty-ninth birthday, she died, alone.

Lady Duff Twysden

LADY Duff Twysden was undoubtedly the most controversial woman in Montparnasse. She was either loved or despised, and some people went from one attitude to another, but no one appeared to be indifferent or neutral about Duff. On the whole there were more men who loved her and women who admired her than there were those who thought her stupid, immoral, affected, predatory, or insincere. Among the latter, however, was the writer Bob McAlmon. "Of the ladies who were on the loose in Montparnasse," he wrote in an unpublished chapter of his memoirs, [Duff] "was the most copied, the least witty or amusing, and she could turn to 'acting her Ladyship' at most dangerous moments." McAlmon's dislike of her was heavily influenced by his dislike, in general, of the British, and particularly members of the British upper classes, although it is true that he admired his in-laws, Lady and Sir John Ellerman, whose daughter, Bryher (née Winifred), he had married. Both Scott and Zelda Fitzgerald had started out by being very much taken with Duff, but something went wrong, and they turned bitterly against her, especially Zelda. For a time Zelda and Duff were both queen bees of Montparnasse, and as in the winged world, two queenbees never get along.

Most people, including myself, thought Duff was delightful. Men fell in love with her on sight, and as for the reaction of women, Nancy Cunard, to whom Duff bore some striking physical and temperamental similarities, provided a tantalizingly evocative portrait:

> She was tall and most elegant of figure, with an exquisite, small head and a dark-haired Eton crop. She had, obviously, *beaucoup de cran* and also *beaucoup de branche*. Noting her equanimity, one felt that she would carry

Lady Duff Twysden, passport photo, 1929 *(Photo courtesy of Professor Carlos Baker).*

off the most difficult and touchy situations. Her shape was lovely, and her figure, the set of her little head, just right, enhanced, as a rule, by a tight-fitting dark blue beret; her thin, well-tailored face, perfect.*

Like many others, I thought Duff was beautiful, captivating, utterly charming. She was tall, almost six feet in high-heeled shoes, had gray eyes, and,

*Nancy Cunard. Letter to Solita Solano (Feb. 1962).

although she was no longer a young girl during her days in Montparnasse, she was a fine figure of a woman. I can picture her now sitting in the Dingo or the Select with a flock of men around her, listening to her every word, loving her looks and her wit and her artistic sensitivity. Some of them doubtless persuaded themselves they were in love with her. Perhaps her most striking feature was her warm and musical voice, which her onetime lover, Harold Loeb, described as "sweet and low." She was instinctively polite toward all she met, and completely without a trace of snobbishness. She was just as friendly and charming to Jimmy the Barman, for instance, as she was to Ernest Hemingway. Whenever she left Jimmy's bar she always went over to say good-bye to him, and she always used the same expression, which I heard her say many times—"Bless you, Jimmy. Bless you." Duff's stylishness many attributed to the simplicity of her clothes, her sparing use of makeup, and that head of close-cropped hair that was as unusual for a woman then as it is now. With all of this she was so obviously sincere and unaffected. She had been educated in England and France. She spoke French almost as well as English, and she could sing in both languages, but she could not be called an intellectual. Above all, people interested her. She wanted to know unusual men and women and have fun with them. She was enchanting, witty, and vivacious.

Duff was already thirty-three when I first knew her in 1925, or perhaps it was the year before. She had been born in London on May 22, 1892, and belonged to a Scottish family named Smurthwaite who had no particular standing in British society. Married twice, first briefly to Lutrell Byrom, and then longer to Sir Roger Twysden, she had produced by the latter a son and heir named Tony. Life following separation from Sir Roger consisted of protracted recriminations generated by Sir Roger and his loyal relatives. Sir Roger had expected his wife to be the ornamental and devoted spouse of an English country squire. Although Duff certainly had the manners and graciousness for such a position, her spirit and desire for adventure were at complete odds with such a boring existence, and, like Nancy Cunard, she eventually fled to Paris where she planned to pursue what she regarded as her real talents—painting, music, and poetry. Regrettably, she never really worked at the development of any of these talents, even though she was a competent pianist and a gifted artist. It was not her style to work. She was made for play.

Her chosen playmate in Paris, or at least the one she traveled with most often, was Pat Guthrie, a former British naval officer, of good family but no observable useful skills. Pat, like Duff, was charming, friendly, polite, softspoken, and, most endearingly, he was utterly without ambition. Everyone liked Pat, even though most agreed he did not have the style that made Duff such a charismatic person. They had, however, one basic difference that could hardly be overlooked by Montparnasse. Whereas Duff could keep going at a party until all the others had dropped by the wayside, drinking one whiskey after another without showing any effects, poor Pat, usually befuddled on his second glass, would retire to a chair where he would sit quietly and eventually fall asleep. I do not remember ever seeing him get noisy or belligerent, though he sometimes could become a little maudlin.

Pat and Duff were devoted to each other and planned to be married as soon as Duff obtained her divorce from Sir Roger, a matter that was taking a considerable time in clearing the British courts. As it stood, both Pat and Duff could count on receiving small but slightly irregular incomes from their families, enough for modest but comfortable living, but in no way sufficient for sprees in Montmartre nightclubs or high-style living at the Ritz. Nonetheless, when they had money, they spent it very easily, and when they were broke, they simply lived on credit. Jimmy the Barman once told me that he was a principal source of credit, but he added that when their money arrived each month, they always paid him in full. They also paid their hotel and other creditors. Fortunately, their fluctuating financial position was well known to their friends, and much of the time it was they who paid the bar checks, the restaurant bills, and the costs of any night life. No repayment was ever expected by friends. It was considered well worth the money just to have Duff and usually Pat, too, along in any party.

Although almost everyone in Montparnasse knew Pat and Duff, two men took a particular interest in her. They were Ernest Hemingway and Harold Loeb. Harold belonged to the Loeb-Guggenheim family of New York, but he was far poorer than many of his wealthy relatives. I guess you would call him an intellectual, since he had published an avant-garde magazine called *Broom*, which had been a modest literary success, but like all the little magazines of that time it had not made any money or even broke even. When Harold's money ran out, or, rather, all that he intended to pump into it, the magazine folded. After that Harold wrote a number of novels which were published without attracting much critical interest. When he met Duff, he was swept off his feet and made a mad play for her. He was deeply in love with her, but even by Harold's own account, she was not with him, although she found him attractive, as did other women. Their brief affair, which Hemingway would mention in *The Sun Also Rises,* ended unhappily for Loeb, but he was by no means ruined by it and afterward he and Duff exchanged friendly letters. Hemingway was also greatly taken by Duff, but he was more restrained in his emotional feelings. He had reached the point when he was at last escaping from the cruel poverty of his early years with Hadley and beginning to enjoy some of the pleasures of life in France. Perhaps Duff was just what he needed, although in view of how he presented her in *The Sun Also Rises* it appears that he was not what Duff needed. Anyway, she created no problem for Hadley. Duff was Hadley's good friend, and Hadley described her as a "very lovely and a very fine lady, very popular and very nice to women, fair and square, a very fine lady." Hemingway and Duff were certainly close friends, and, with Pat, Duff went many places with the Hemingways.

One of the places they went to together was to the annual seven-day fiesta of San Fermin in Pamplona in the Basque region of northern Spain. It was to be a "fun party," and the four of them were joined by Donald Ogden Stewart, then at the height of his career as a humor writer, and by Bill Smith, a longtime friend of Hemingway from his days back in Michigan. It was this week in Pamplona that Hemingway used as the basis for *The Sun Also Rises*. "It was on the train to Madrid that I felt the urge to make this adventure into my first effort at writing a novel," he told me in 1933 in Paris. "I couldn't wait and I started to write it in the hotel as soon as we arrived."

There was plenty of drama in the actual events in Pamplona he could use as background: the running of the bulls through the streets of the town in the early morning hours; the mock fights, entertaining but also dangerous, that would-be "matadors" performed inside the bullring with young cows whose horns were wrapped in burlap; the dancing in the streets and squares that went on night and day; the frenzied drinking and eating; the parades and the colorful conglomeration of Spaniards and foreigners on holiday; and, above all, the bullfights themselves that began promptly each afternoon at six. Besides the pageantry, he had the emotional strains that permeated his little group and which he could build upon and exaggerate into novel form, little realizing what effect his book would have on the lives of the real people who served as models for his fictional characters.

To start with, there was Duff, of whom Donald Ogden Stewart said: "It was hard not to be in love with Duff because she was so beautiful and attractive." Duff was with Pat Guthrie, of course, but only a couple of weeks before that, she had gone to St. Jean de Luz with Harold Loeb, and everyone knew it. Furthermore, Loeb himself was in Pamplona, deeply resentful at having been cast aside and now having to watch her back with Pat. Yet he did not leave. If Hemingway had wished to create a "situation," he could not have found a better one, but the evidence seems to show that all this came about almost accidentally. Duff was, of course, the heroine of the novel, and Loeb was the villain. As Duff said about Loeb's fictional counterpart Robert Cohn, "He is not one of us."

This expression was an actual favorite with Duff. She has been accused of using it to assert a class snobbishness, but it really had a somewhat different meaning to her. It was by way of being her philosophy of life. She believed in certain "true values" of which love between a man and a woman, based on mutual trust, intense interest in each other's welfare, kindness, politeness, and a kind of "oneness" were the key factors. "Us" usually included persons who were not necessarily emotionally involved, but whose philosophy of life had the same basis. Under no circumstances was this classification intended to include people of the same social standing, or who had great wealth, or who were recognized in the arts of some other field. Jimmy the Barman, for example, was one of us, but Harold Loeb was not, while Hemingway was, as well as Hadley and many others. It would be oversimplifying the expression to say that "us" included all her friends, for it also admitted fictional characters, people she knew about but did not know. She had thought Loeb one of us at the beginning, but after her little affair with him, according to Loeb's own account, she decided that he was not.

As he sat down to write the first draft of his novel, which he originally called *Fiesta*, a title that was actually used in the English edition, Hemingway must have planned to write a roman à clef, for he concentrated on his friends' superficial characteristics and barely changed their names. Lady Duff Twysden became Lady Brett Ashley; Harold Loeb became Robert Cohn; Bill Smith combined with Donald Stewart and became Bill Gorton; Pat Guthrie became Mike Campbell; and Hemingway himself, the narrator of the novel, became Jake Barnes, a journalist. Hadley was not included in the cast. Each person he described in such a way that one could hardly fail to recognize the original models. But there the likeness stopped. He refused to portray any, or many, of their positive characteristics, giving them instead either unattractive or skin-deep qualities, the most notable example being Robert Cohn, the "boxing champion of Princeton."

What was his motive in all this? It is hard to say with any clear assurance, but it is certain that even by the mid-twenties Hemingway harbored some sort of resentment against many of the people of Montparnasse, both men and women. He told this to me and others on several occasions. "I'm going to get even with those bastards," he said to me in 1933, the year of Gertrude Stein's best-seller, *The Autobiography of Alice B. Toklas*, where his erstwhile friend called him "ninety percent Rotarian." And in the same conversation he emphasized that *The Sun Also Rises* was a novel, not a gossipy report. I was writing a novel, he told me, and if resemblances between his characters and real persons and events existed, it was purely coincidental. He was obviously annoyed that so much fuss had been made about "the six characters in search of an author—with a gun." He enjoyed needling people, enjoyed ranting about people he disliked. I think he even enjoyed disliking them. Sometimes he would pound the table and become very emotional over something that was long since past and not really very important in any case. Even earlier he had hinted that an awful reckoning lay ahead. Perhaps it was *A Moveable Feast* that he had in mind, for in those posthumously published sketches of life in Paris in the 1920s he scornfully rejected many with whom he was once on friendly terms. Doubtless what I heard him say in the early 1930s was a sign of the paranoia that later was to be his complete undoing.

But in 1925 Hemingway was very anxious indeed to write a successful novel, one that would bring him money and recognition. Making his first effort a roman à clef was perhaps a device to this end. It would have succeeded anyway, but the controversy between him and the models who served for his fictional characters lasted on and on and continues even today, even though almost all of them are dead.

Besides the five who journeyed to Pamplona, Hemingway presented several other Montparnassians in the early chapters set in Paris, namely Ford Madox Ford as Braddocks, Harold Stearns as Harvey Stone, Kitty Cannell as Frances Clyne, and Glenway Wescott as Robert Prentice. When the book was published in 1926 it caused a furor in Montparnasse. Indigation against the author flared on all sides. Loeb was pictured as a brute, an ass, utterly insensitive, and so stupid that all he wanted to do after beating up a man half his size was to shake hands with him to show that there were no hard feelings. Harold was not the most popular man in Montparnasse, yet no one failed to see the injustice of Hemingway's portrayal, and no one who knew Harold Loeb could miss the identification.

But when Hemingway portrayed Harold's mistress as Frances Clyne, no one dreamed that she was meant to characterize the real-life Kitty Cannell, except for his statement that Frances was Cohn's longtime companion. The Frances of the novel had only one characteristic in common with the real Kitty—they were both tall.

Kitty Cannell and Harold Loeb had a great personal attachment to the Hemingway family. They went on trips together, they often dined together, and Loeb had not only a personal admiration for and trust in Hemingway, but he believed in his talent as a writer. Furthermore, they played tennis together, and sometimes boxed.

On the other hand, Kitty did not care so much for Hemingway, whom she considered rather crude in speech and manners, but she, like so many of us,

felt a great affection for Hadley. So Kitty tolerated Ernest for Hadley's sake, and I guess Hem tolerated Kitty for the sake of his friendship with his tennis partner. He even went so far as to tell her he would some day write a book in which many of the characters of Montparnasse would be portrayed, but promised that she would not be among them.

I, for one, liked Kitty Cannell very much, and so did my wife with whom she had a particular friendship. But we did not care so much for Loeb, so the two families rarely got together, though Kitty and Hadley and my wife often met for tea in the afternoon. Kitty was born of an American father and an English mother, who as a widow moved to Paris in the twenties. Kitty had therefore spent much of her youth in Paris and spoke the language fluently. She was also well acquainted with French literature and art, her special interest being the surrealists and their forerunners. Kitty did a little writing, mostly articles and some fashion reviews, but she had no marked success in this field, probably because she did not devote herself to the grind of literary work. Or perhaps she did not really have the gift.

She was a rather quiet woman with a soft voice, a gentle manner and sharp insight into the character of people around her. She was good looking, even handsome, without being beautiful. She could be warm and affectionate, but she could also be objective. She was admired by many, especially men, but often at a distance.

When Kitty Cannell appeared in print as Frances Clyne, she was astonished. At first she was inclined to laugh it off as a bad joke played by a writer who vaunted his crude language and ill manners. Then she began to notice that others, new acquaintances, began to treat her in a somewhat different manner, or even avoided her or kept her at a distance. And then she became angry and bitter. Her friends gathered around her and were highly indignant at the way Hem had treated her. I think she took it too seriously, magnifying something that should have been laughed away or at least shrugged off. He had portrayed her as a rapacious female, a gold digger, a fierce man chaser, an "exploiter" of Robert Cohn, determined to marry him come hell or high water, a harpy, a torturer armed with sarcastic words. Poor Kitty!

And yet, a few years before her death in Boston in the seventies, Kitty wrote of Hem in the days before success had enveloped him, before he had chosen to adopt the myth of "Papa": "He looked straight at me with what I called his shining morning face—rosy cheeked, with white teeth and that sudden marvelous smile of a good little eight-year-old boy. It made you feel like giving him an apple—or maybe your heart."

Duff, perhaps understandably, received better treatment. She was portrayed as an attractive woman, but Hemingway also created the impression that she was promiscuous and that she played fast and loose with the hearts of men who loved her. In later years Hemingway told A. E. Hotchner many

Kathleen Cannell, journalist, Paris fashion editor for the *New York Times* from 1931 to 1940, photographed in the 1940s *(Photo from the collection of Morrill Cody).*

downright lies about Duff which painted her as a nymphomaniac and a thoroughly unprincipled creature. How Hemingway, whom we had all liked and admired so much in his youth, could have done such things is hard to believe and even harder to understand. That his mind was diseased is the only possible answer I can find.

While Harold was deeply hurt and thoroughly angry at the way he had been portrayed in the novel, and is said to have vowed to beat up Hemingway if he ever found him, Duff took the matter in her stride. "He was writing a novel and he had the right to do anything with his characters that he wished," she said. Later, however, when she saw that people around her were judging her more insistently by Hemingway's characterization than by her own natural traits, she too became hurt and angered.

The only person who comes out clean and pure among the Montparnassians is the narrator of the novel, Jake Barnes, presumably a portrait of Hemingway. What a coincidence!

After the Pamplona fiesta Duff did not go directly back to Paris, and when she did, she found that Pat, angry at her infidelity with Loeb, had deserted her for an American girl, a liaison which did not last long. Friends of Pat and Duff tried to get them together again. We all felt that this couple had so much in common and somehow symbolized "true love." We could not let them fall

Pencil sketch by Duff Twysden King, about 1936, showing her husband Clinton King, two unidentified children, and herself. The locale is Texas where the Kings lived in the 1930s. According to friends John and Maria Rogers, who were among others to receive the sketch as a Christmas message, the likeness of Duff is quite good (Photo courtesy of Professor Carlos Baker).

apart. I remember one evening in Jimmy's Trois et As bar when Duff sat at one end of the long bar and Pat at the other, she in tears, he glum. Moving back and forth between them were various friends, including myself, who were trying to persuade them to talk to each other "for a few minutes, just to say hello." Each adamantly refused and so that was that. This was before the novel came out.

And then not long afterward, in July 1927, Duff met a handsome, young and delightful American boy, some twelve years her junior. His name was Clinton King. "I saw Duff in a big mirror behind Jimmy's bar and immediately, but at once, fell in love with her," he told me later. "She said she fell in love with me too at the same moment." It was a glorious union, and she was certainly happier with "George," as she always called Clinton, than she would have been with Pat, who had a drug problem which led him to take his life about a year later. Duff and Clinton King were married as soon as Duff's divorce came through. They went to live in Mexico in a house overlooking Lake Chapala, but later moved to New City, New York, and after that to Santa Fe, where Duff contracted consumption and died. They had had eleven joyous years together, King told me on several occasions. But even in death Hemingway was to haunt her memory with cruel and malicious lies about her funeral and burial. He spread it around that the pallbearers were all her former lovers, an obvious fiction since she was cremated and there was no burial service. Maybe he was still piqued that other men had been closer to Duff than he had been. And maybe the words the fictional Duff says on the last page of his novel to Jake Barnes were actually similar to words she at one time said to him: "Oh, Jake . . . we could have had such a damned good time together." Whatever had gone wrong between them, Hemingway never forgot it.

The Beautiful and the Loving

THE young women who took up the modeling profession in Paris in the twenties generally came from farmer or small-town families, poor but honest, and almost always distant from the city. They were attracted by the fact that posing was not a hard skill to learn even though it was often boring and tiring to stand in the nude for an hour at a time. It was also sometimes chilly despite the efforts of the school managers to keep up the temperature. Fears caused by personal modesty were quickly overcome when they saw that the painters were truly interested in their work and not given to gawking at them. Furthermore, the pay was better than that of a shop assistant, and they enjoyed the free and easy contact with the painters and sculptors. They were always meeting new people. Any day might bring a new adventure. It was certainly better than working on that old, scratchy farm, milking cows, or picking apples. Of course they did not tell their parents they were going to Paris to be models. They said they would stay with a friend and look for a job as a salesgirl or waitress in a restaurant. Each girl would receive serious advice from her mother on how to avoid contact with boys who might try to take advantage of them. All promised to write often and they usually did. Each model dutifully reported back that she had a job in a shop and that she was sharing a small apartment with several other girls. This last was usually true, for the model almost always kept a *pied-à-terre* even though they might not pass every night in it.

A new model usually started her career by posing in one of the academies, where many of the artists gathered daily to sketch or paint from one of the models of the day or week. The academies were not, strictly speaking, schools, but rather facilities where the artist could work out his own techniques and trends. Usually there was a professor or established artist who

Jacqueline, age 18, model for Man Ray, Paris, 1930s *(Photo courtesy of Juliet Man Ray).*

came in Saturday morning to look over the week's work of each student and to make suggestions to him, sometimes to compliment him. But no student was obliged to receive this criticism. He could be absent on Saturday morning and many were.

Friendships grew easily between students and the models. One day, after a model had finished posing and was dressed again, a boy might ask her to have a coffee with him at a neighboring café. If she were not otherwise engaged, she might accept, and one thing might lead to another. He would invite her to dinner, and before long he would invite her to his studio for a night of lovemaking. But such proceedings were not promiscuous as they might seem on the surface. The girls, all of the models as far as I know, had the same code of morals. They went with a boy because they were in love with him, at least for the moment. As long as a girl was attached to one boy she never flirted with another, and she was never unfaithful to him. I suppose there were exceptions to this rule, but I never heard of one. Either party was free to break off the relationship at any time with no recriminations. Very often the model only came to the artist's studio two or three times a week. The other nights she spent in her own *pied-à-terre*. Under no circumstances did she accept money, as such, from her boyfriend, although she would accept an occasional gift and

Unknown model, Paris, mid-1920s *(Photo from the collection of Morrill Cody)*.

Vivian, child of Montparnasse, singer, pianist, and model *(Photo from the collection of Morrill Cody)*.

meals, of course. Sometimes such a couple formed a more or less permanent liaison, and sometimes the two were eventually married. But the model was not hunting a husband, or at least she did not seem to be, though perhaps there was a little hope that marriage was somewhere on the horizon. The worst insult that you could offer a model was to imply in any way that she had some faint relationship to a prostitute.

An American friend of mine had a lovely girl named Daniele, who came to visit him in his studio two or three times a week, and they were very happy

Jannine, Paris model, about 1927 *(Photo from the collection of Morrill Cody).*

together. He wanted her to live with him in the studio and to pose for him when he was not working at one of the academies, but she would not.

"You would get bored with me," she said.

"I would not. I love to have you around, and I want to paint your beautiful body. You will make me a famous artist." But she would not, though it was obvious that she was crazy about him.

Then one day she disappeared. He asked for her at the academie. She had not been seen. He looked for her in the cafés. And one day another model told him that Daniele had returned to her parents in Belgium. She did not know the address or even the name of the town. Too bad.

Two years passed, and he had made a new attachment. Daniele began to fade in his mind. Then one day he saw her in the street. She tried to avoid him but he caught up with her.

"What happened to you? Where have you been? Let us sit in this café, and you will tell me what happened. I looked all over for you."

"Poor Joe! I was sorry to leave you that way, but I had to return to my parents in Belgium. I was pregnant!"

"Pregnant! With my child?"

"Who else's, monsieur!" Daniele was very indignant. "Of course it was your baby, a boy with blue eyes like yours and your nose. I named him Jean-Pierre. He was a darling. I hated to give him up."

"Give him up?"

"Of course. You did not want married life with a baby to take care of, and I couldn't do it alone. So I put him out for adoption, and he was taken by a fine couple in the town who could not have children of their own. The man was a garage mechanic whose father owned the establishment. Some day it will be the son's. His wife worked in shop, but she gave that up when the adoption was completed. They were fine people."

"I would have liked to see him."

She rose to her feet. "I must go now. I have a boyfriend I love very much. He has even asked me to marry him, and perhaps I will. I do not know whether I am ready for marriage, but I am a little tired of modeling. If you see me with a man you may wave to me, but don't let him see any possessiveness. Good-bye. You are a fine man." And she was off. He never saw her again, but he often thought about his son in Belgium.

ROSALIE AND CARMEN

Over the door was a flowing sign in the romantic flowered lettering of the Belle Epoque. It read ROSALIE. There was no indication of the character of the establishment beyond the door, no posted menu of the restaurant. Just the word ROSALIE, but most of the writers and artists of Paris in the twenties and earlier knew it was there and came at least occasionally to dine and meet their friends. Rosalie's restaurant stood at 13 rue Campagne Première, a small street that connects the Boulevard Montparnasse with the Boulevard Raspail.

Opening the door of Rosalie's one was often greeted with a pungent odor of fried onions and garlic, since the room inside had little ventilation. However, this in no way discouraged the customers who were not seeking the refinements of *haute cuisine bourgeoise*. One stepped down from the street level to the dark tiled floor. The room was big enough for several long wooden tables flanked by rough and hard wooden benches without backs each of which accommodated up to eight persons if they were thin and sat close together.

At the far end was a door leading into the kitchen, and over it reposed a large slate which proclaimed the menu for the day. There were usually three or

Rosalie Tabia, model for Whistler and benefactor of Modigliani, in Chez Rosalie, rue Campagne Ìière, Paris, about 1930 *(Photo from the collection of Morrill Cody).*

four hors d' oeuvres such as a tomato salad, a portion of smoked herring, a pâté, and the inevitable hard-boiled egg with mayonnaise. The main courses were usually stews or sometimes roasts, along with one fish offering. Vegetables were served separately and after the meat course, as was generally customary in restaurants in those days. A couple of items of cheese, including Petit Suisse with jam and a few desserts such as crème caramel or mousse au chocolat finished the list. If, in the early twenties, you took three items from this offering and a quarter bottle of wine the bill rarely went above one franc, though you could live it up with extra wine or a cheese *and* a dessert and make it reach a franc fifty. Rosalie served no coffee because she did not want her customers to sit around taking up space that would be better used by eaters. "Go to the Rotonde for your coffee," she would say. "That's where you will find all the talkers and loafers." The Rotonde was a big café on the Boulevard Montparnasse.

Rosalie herself, her gray curly hair flying, took the orders, cooked the meals, served the clients, and provided them with a steady flow of gossip and commentary about the quarter, her views on the politics of the day, and humorous stories she had heard from other folk not present. Everyone was welcome if he or she looked reasonably poor. "Rosalie's restaurant is for poor students and artists," she would proclaim, and when some unfortunate girl, usually an American, appeared at the door in a fur coat, no matter how ratty, Rosalie would push her and her friends out without ceremony. "Go away, rich people," she would shout. "Rosalie does not serve the rich, only the poor!" No argument would soften her heart, even though the restaurant might be two-thirds empty.

Then one day, Rosalie changed her opinion because she had heard about an economic recession in the United States. Now she was sorry for the rich people who no longer had any money, and so she began to welcome the fur-coated women with open arms. "Come in, you poor people," she would say. "I know what you are suffering. You can eat cheaply at Rosalie's. Have anything you want and don't worry about *l'addition*."

But the supply of poor artists was constant and immediately at hand, for the rue Compagne Première and nearby streets were full of artists' studios, with a veritable rabbit warren of them at number 9. This building, which still stands today, contains over one hundred small studios which were constructed with the doors, windows, and leftover material salvaged from the Paris Exhibition of 1889. Here the Italian painter Amedeo Modigliani lived briefly as he had at number 3. Because he rarely paid his rent, he moved often.

All the biographies of Modigliani sing the praises of Rosalie Tabia, not so much as a model but rather as a benefactor of the eccentric and slightly mad artist. She fed him when the others rejected his paintings and drawings, and his friends became fed up with his exaggeraged drinking scenes. He fought with Rosalie, too, but he knew that he could always turn to her in an hour of need.

As a sort of repayment for her motherly kindness, Modigliani painted frescoes with figures and scenes on several of her plastered walls, and when he committed suicide in 1920, dealers paid her handsomely for the right to remove these works. She then proclaimed that she had known all along that he was a great painter. Some other paintings of his on canvas had been "stored" in the cellar of the restaurant but, when brought to light, were found to have been good eating for the rats.

Rosalie had known other painters, too, and particularly the great Whistler, for whom she posed in her younger days. She said she had always liked Whistler. One proof of it seemed to be the remarkable likeness of Rosalie's son, Luigi, to the American painter. "Yes," she would say, "my son does look like Whistler, doesn't he?" And her face would be diffused with a warm and wistful smile.

Rosalie must have posed for Whistler in the 1892–95 period when he had his studio on the roof at 86 rue Notre Dame des Champs and his residence facing the garden at the back of 110 rue de Bac, both of which are largely unchanged since his day. Whistler's door was famous for its bright blue color and shiny brass knocker. She had a bundle of Whistler's drawings which she said he had given her, but these too had been badly mutilated by her cellar rats. Rosalie also said she had posed for Cézanne, but this was harder to prove.

Rosalie's restaurant in the later twenties became more and more a favorite of the American Left Bank tourists who were beginning to invade Montparnasse. One day a couple of schoolteachers, carried away with the mood of the

Interior of Rosalie's restaurant, rue Campagne Iière, Paris, about 1930 *(Photo from the collection of Morrill Cody).*

times, offered to buy her restaurant at a price she could not refuse. She appeared to be delighted at the prospect of retirement and turned over the key as soon as the purchase price was safely in hand. The American women immediately cleaned up the place, repainted the walls, hired a cook and a waitress, and replaced the plain wooden tables and benches with nice bright and shinier new ones. Rosalie suggested that the old tables and benches be placed in the cellar where they would be out of the way. Within days the customers began to drop off, and in a month there were none at all, for neither the artists nor the tourists wanted Rosalie's without Rosalie and her plain wooden tables, blackboard menu, and, above all, her rollicking humor.

So Rosalie agreed to buy it back for one tenth of the sale price, brought up the wooden tables and benches from the cellar, marked up the slate in her almost illegible handwriting, and in a few days the place was as full as ever. Word of mouth traveled fast in those days.

Incredible as it may seem, Rosalie, who was a shrewd business woman, despite her generosity, repeated this same scenario with two more gullible American women a couple of years later, and again she bought the restaurant back when it failed to hold its customers under "foreign" rule. There were the same "new" tables and chairs which she had thoughtfully placed in the cellar when the first purchasers had left. Now she sold them to the new owners at a considerable profit, replacing them once again with the old wooden tables and benches when she returned to take over the management.

Then about 1932, when the flow of star-struck bohemian Americans and starving artists began to dwindle, Rosalie finally retired for good on the profits of her labors as a *restaurantrice*. Today, the premises are occupied by a shiny plastic snack bar, and the girl behind the counter has never heard of Rosalie.

If the biographers of Whistler failed to mention Rosalie, they lavished plenty of words on Carmen Rossi, another old model who was well known to the Montparnassians of the twenties, for she had not only posed for the great man but had actually been in a sort of partnership with him as the manager of the Academie Whistler at 6 Passage Stanislas, now called rue Jules Chaplain, just around the corner from Whistler's studio on the rue Notre Dame des Champs.

All Whistler's biographers say that his appreciation of Carmen was very warm. He thought she was fun to have around, and he admired her wit as well as her beauty. I did not see her until she was old, but it was not hard to imagine that she might have been very attractive when she was young. There is no doubt that Whistler was very fond of her and encouraged her to start an academy where young painters could work together and learn from each other. He gave her some two hundred pounds (no mean sum in those days) to rent, refurbish, and equip the building with easels, stools, and model stands. It was to be called the Academie Carmen, but when the sign went up it said Academie Whistler. When he saw it, however, he protested, and she was forced to change the name.

Whistler came to the academy frequently, sometimes every day, to discuss his theories of painting with the students, to comment on their work, and as a result it had an immediate success, taking students away from the other academies by the dozen.

Alas, Carmen's abilities did not lie in the field of administration, and the school suffered greatly from lack of organization and discipline. Nevertheless, it succeeded greatly, no doubt mainly because of the attention Whistler lavished on it. When he moved back to London, however, and only came to Paris very occasionally, its appeal gradually slipped away.

Also, Whistler was troubled by the disappearance of many of his drawings, paintings, and sketches. He suspected that Carmen was helping herself, but he could never prove it. Certainly someone was stealing his work because from time to time some of the sketches turned up in the hands of local dealers. When Whistler died Carmen produced a considerable number of his works which she said he had given her in return for her posing, or simply because she liked them. She immediately sold them for a goodly sum to an American collector, and they can be seen today as part of the Freer Collection in the Smithsonian Institution in Washington.

Carmen's academy faded away after a couple of years, and she went back to modeling. In fact, she was still a model when I knew her in the twenties, and she posed for me on one occasion.

Like Rosalie, Carmen was of Italian origin, despite her Spanish given name. She was a little older than Rosalie. The two women vied for general attention, and little warmth existed between them. Carmen spoke of Rosalie as that "restaurant woman." Rosalie would speak of "that Spaniard" and make fun of the pretentions of Carmen "just because she once had an art school. After all, I knew Whistler better than she did." And I guess she did.

KIKI OF MONTPARNASSE

The most famous model of her day, or perhaps any day, was Kiki. A simple peasant girl from Burgundy, she had a tremendous lust for life, for fun and song, human emotions, and love. Hemingway called her the queen of Montparnasse. I think it would be more accurate to call her the spirit, the animator of the quarter. For a number of years, she breathed fire into many gatherings, she stirred the blood of all who knew her, men and women alike.

Named Alice Prin at birth, she had spent her early years with her grandmother and grandfather and five cousins of about the same age. The grandparents eked out a bare living in a remote village of the great wine country. These five children were the offspring of the three daughters the grandmother had borne. All were illegitimate, and their three mothers had all left to find their fortune in Paris. Grandma was elected to bring them up, and she did her best. "We were six little love babies," Kiki used to say. Kiki's mother, who had a job in Paris, sent five francs (a dollar) a month for her support.

At twelve, Kiki's mother sent for her, and for a short time she lived at home and went to school, but at thirteen she gave up school for good and spent the next year or two in a series of poorly paid jobs and in profound discord with her mother and her mother's lover. One day her mother put her out, and she was on her own. She tried many jobs, but before long she turned to modeling as her only way to earn a modest living. She was a beautiful girl with a beautiful body. She had a lovely oval face, wide set, dark eyes, dark hair which was bobbed in the fashion of the day, and white even teeth, and a very happy smile. Her lips, which Man Ray later immortalized on canvas, were full but not sensual. Her face was always heavily made up, stage fashion. She had only one blemish about which she complained bitterly: she had no pubic hair.

Today, portraits of Kiki decorate the walls of many museums, although her name does not usually appear on the brass plate below the painting or sculpture. It is my opinion that the name of the model should be immortalized as well as that of the artist, but no one seems to agree with me. She posed for Soutine, Kisling, Foujita, Utrillo, Man Ray, Pascin, and probably Modigliani—and of course for many other artists who are less renowned. She lived with some of them. She and Soutine, for instance, lived together for almost a year, and he did many portraits of her.

Then she met the American painter and photographer Man Ray, and it was love at first sight for both of them. She hesitated to pose for photographs at first because of her "physical blemish," until he promised to keep it secret from the camera. Man Ray saw her as she was, a simple, untutored girl with a

Carmen Rossi, Whistler's model and companion, Paris, about 1930 *(Photo from the collection of Morrill Cody).*

Kiki, actress, writer, model, and painter, whose personality became a symbol of life in Montparnasse, 1924 *(Photo from the collection of Morrill Cody).*

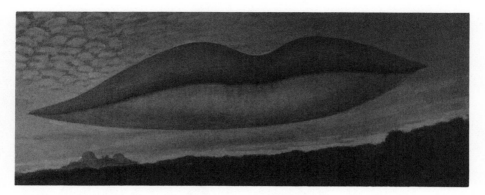

Observatory Time—The Lovers (1932–34), painting by Man Ray *(Photo courtesy of Juliet Man Ray).*

Sketch of Kiki by Foujita, Japanese artist, Paris, 1929, with inscription (top) from Foujita to Flossie Martin, who owned the book in which this sketch appeared *(Photo from the collection of Morrill Cody).*

natural gift for self-expression, a child of nature who had more to offer than most of the people around her. With Man she was able to bring out her talents in unexpected ways. She gave up posing for anyone else; she began to sing some of the rough and bawdy Burgundy ballads she had learned as a child; she began to paint with some success, although she had never had a lesson in her life; and she was one of the first to make collages. She exhibited in Paris and London and sold many of her works. She eventually wrote her autobiography in a colorful French all her own. This book had a great success in both French

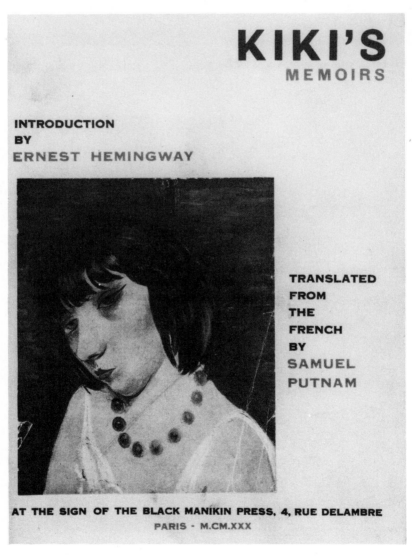

Title page and portrait of Kiki from *Kiki's Memoirs*, Black Manikin Press, Paris, 1930.

and an English translation by Samuel Putnam, with an introduction (a poor one) by Ernest Hemingway. Without Man Ray it is hard to imagine how she would have developed these creative outpourings, for he was a person of great understanding. I knew him for more than forty-five years, and he was one of the sweetest and most intelligent persons I have ever known. He and Marcel Duchamp, his great friend, had this characteristic in common. Man Ray lavished love and attention on Kiki, and she lavished her love on him. Their life together was not entirely a bed of roses, however, because she was sometimes jealous, without reason I think, and threw tantrums in public that were the talk of Montparnasse. These emotional outbursts were never in private and that may be a small key to part of her character.

It should be noted that after two or three years of regular meals and good food with Man Ray her "blemish" was, shall we say, overcome. There was in those days a night spot on the Boulevard Montparnasse called "The Jockey" where many of us gathered in the evening to dance to the music of Hilaire Hiler at the piano, or simply to sit and drink. Hiler, an American painter and musician, had decorated the outside of the building with cowboy scenes. These same paintings were later moved across the boulevard to another building where they can be found today. "The Jockey" was in the building now occupied by Regine's "New Jimmy's."

Hilaire Hiler was a remarkably warm and friendly man who took a great personal interest in all he met and is remembered today with fondness by those who have survived the intervening years. And to "The Jockey" came most of the art and literary folk of the quarter, with Man Ray and Kiki among the first. Kiki loved it at once and from that time on took up a stand there night after night. If Man was out with clients or friends, she would come alone, and he could pick her up there later in the evening. It was here that she started to sing her Burgundy ballads with such success that soon the place was crowded with many tourists and persons from other parts of the city. While her voice was untrained, she sang with such spirit and verve that she charmed everyone. Soon she began to know many of the literary people as well as the artists. Jean Cocteau was particularly taken with her simple approach to the problems of life, and she recognized in him the same simplicity. Ernest Hemingway also took a great interest in her. Many admirers tried to lure her away from Man Ray, but she was deaf to all such offers. If she ever left "The Jockey" without him, it was to go directly home and wait for his arrival.

Then one day she left Man Ray and joined a French writer, Henri Broca, who had been helping her with her memoirs. The six-year liaison was over, although they remained friends and she would drop in to see him in his studio from time to time. It was shortly after this that her memoirs were published by Edward Titus, the husband of Helena Rubinstein, the purveyor of cosmetics. He ran a bookshop called "At the Sign of the Black Manikin" in the rue Delambre and published books under the same name. Kiki's memoirs were banned in the United States, but that only made them more attractive to the tourists. Later, in a somewhat altered version, they appeared in America and

Man Ray, surrealist painter, photographer, and his wife, Juliet, Paris, 1959 (*Photo from the collection of Morrill Cody*).

had a considerable success. Kiki had more money in her pocket than she had ever dreamed of. But she spent it easily, or gave it away. She had no basic interest in money beyond the need for food and lodging. She was a selfless person, and that, too, was part of her charm.

But from the time she left Man Ray, her glory began to fade. Without him she was like an orchestra without a conductor, or an airplane without a pilot. But also Montparnasse itself began to fade. American and British residents were returning home and the tourists were dwindling in number. By 1935 Montparnasse was no longer an attraction and with the approach of war it ceased to exist as a real art colony. Kiki survived the war, but she was ill with dropsy and other complications. She had lost her figure, but she retained her oval face still heavily covered with makeup. She died shortly after the war. She was forty-seven.

Mary Reynolds and Gala Eluard

IN the summer months, many of the artists and writers of Montparnasse left Paris to the tourists and found some quiet and inexpensive spot where they could work or perhaps simply rest and swim and relax. In the summer of 1933, a group of us went to the little fishing village of Cadaques in the extreme northeast corner of Spain, close to the French frontier. It was one of the most enjoyable and stimulating summers I ever spent anywhere, mostly because of the fascinating people who were my companions. In those days Cadaques was not the fashionable tourist center that it has become today. It was a simple little fishing port dominated by a handsome, massive church which overlooked the town from a small hill. The economy was based on a canning factory for anchovies, then plentiful in the Mediterranean waters. There was also some activity in the production of red wine from the grapes that grew in abundance on the neighboring hills. The only "foreigners" there were a few citizens from Barcelona, from nearby France, and from the mainline town of Figueras, where one got off the train to take the bus to the coast. The village boasted one rather moth-eaten hotel and a "fonda," or pensione, which was clean and pleasant, but decidedly lacking in modern facilities.

Our group consisted of Mary Louise Reynolds, a handsome American intellectual, a distinguished resident of Montparnasse since 1921. She is perhaps best remembered for her close friendship with Marcel Duchamp, the Frenchman who painted *Nude Descending a Staircase*, for her love of cats, and for her talents as a bookbinder and book designer. She is also remembered as the historian of the surrealist movement. Mary had collected every book, every catalogue, every scrap of paper that had ever been printed about this revolu-

One man and five women pose to be photographed. From left to right; Gala Dali, unknown, Marcel Duchamp, Mary Reynolds, Virginia Poeter, unknown. Near Cadaques, Costa Brava, Spain, 1933 *(Photo from the collection of Morrill Cody).*

tionary art and literary movement, a monumental task, but one of great affection, for she was a friend of everyone who belonged to that artistic surge led by André Breton and of which Marcel Duchamp was one of the founding fathers. Among Mary's closest friends were Jean Cocteau, Raymond Queneau, Francis Picabia, Juan Miró, Tristan Tzara, Alexander Calder, Louis Aragon, Hans Arp, Max Ernst, and Jacques Baron. Today, Mary's splendid surrealist collection is housed in the Art Institute of Chicago.

The surrealist movement in art and literature began to take form in the mind of its most ardent leader, André Breton, in the early twenties. By 1924 it had become a full-fledged and recognized intellectual religion. Much of its earliest success was due to the intensity and determination of its leader. André Breton craved to be a master among men with a devoted cluster of disciples around him.

In substance, surrealism was based on the operations of the subconscious mind. Daydreams and nightmares were remembered and written down, or captured in drawings and paintings. This was the expression of that unknown world under sleep or perhaps hypnosis. The more fantastic the hallucination the more interesting the literary or artistic expression. This led to magnificent flights of imagination such as those found in the paintings of Dali or Max Ernst, or in the writing of Desnos and Eluard. One phase of the movement was "automatic writing." A group would meet in a café where each, equipped with pencil and paper, would sit down and write frantically and at the greatest possible speed everything that entered his mind, without sequences or structure or discipline. The results were often decidedly Freudian eroticism. The automatic writing bug gave out rather rapidly though, but many tried it, even Picasso, although he was not a true disciple of surrealism.

Aside from its artistic expression, surrealism also carried the torch of antisocial freedom, as so many movements have before it. "Down with the stupid bourgeois morality," "Down with armies and politicians and the rich, unless they are artists and writers"—such were the slogans. This was fun too, but it was not what attracted the avant-garde. The focal point was the discovery that the occult could be a fine source of inventiveness and heretofore almost unknown flights of fancy. One began seeing paintings showing nudes with the heads of animals, birds with the heads of beautiful women, grotesque creatures that breathed fire or exhibited bodily shapes resembling nothing anyone had ever before seen. That many of these ideas were reminiscent of the paintings of the fifteenth-century Dutch and German artists was inconsequential, since these creatures were in no way copies of the old masters. All this was fun, great fun, and everyone enjoyed it. What a considerable and welcome change it was from the overseriousness of the cubists and other movements that had preceded surrealism. Despite the comic tendencies that infected surrealism, the quality of the painting and sculpture was remarkable.

In the long run most of the surrealists—Duchamp, Dali, Ernst—moved away from Breton. Although they accused him of trying to make himself a dictator, they never abandoned the principles he had developed.

At Cadaques that summer, too, was Marcel Duchamp, a man of great depth and talent, who was my longtime friend. Mary Reynolds was dying to marry Marcel, but he would not do so, although he was devoted to her and their liaison went on for many years. Certainly at that time in Montparnasse the two most attractive men were Duchamp and Max Ernst, one a Frenchman, the other a German. Both were gentle, soft-voiced, soft-mannered intellectuals with a quiet force of character underneath their gentle manners. Both eventually lived in the United States and became citizens. The girls adored them and they adored the girls, and both could have married any woman they wanted. Undoubtedly Marcel was deeply attached to Mary. The reason he refused to marry her may have been that in 1925 he had married Lydie Sarrasan-Levassor. The marriage had turned out very badly indeed, though for what reason I do not know. They separated after a couple of months and this may have soured him on marriage. He already knew Mary at this time. Or it may be that he simply wanted to have his separate residence, as indeed he always maintained. In his own place he could hang his chess games on the wall, and receive his male cronies. I am inclined to think it was the latter. In later years, however, he did marry and was very happy with his wife, Tina.

The other members of the group that summer at Cadaques were Virginia Poeter, a pianist from New York, a gay and companionable young woman, and Man Ray, the American surrealist painter and widely known photographer and likewise a close friend. We had gone to Cadaques in the first place at the suggestion of Salvador Dali and his companion, Elena Eluard, nicknamed

Mary Louise Reynolds, American art historian, supporter and friend of Marcel
Duchamp, in Spain, near Cadaques, 1933 *(Photo from the collection of Morrill
Cody).*

Virginia Poeter, American pianist, and Jopie Wilson, Montparnasse, 1932 *(Photo
from the collection of Morrill Cody).*

Gala, who later became his wife. Dali knew this region of Spain well, for he
had been born in nearby Figueras in 1904. His father was a notary, a high
position in the social structure of Spain, a sort of manager of financial affairs,
estates, inheritances with semilegal authority. He was a notable in his community and he also was well known in Cadaques because he owned a fine
summer house there.

Early on, Salvador Dali had taken a great interest in drawing and painting.
He had gone to school in Figueras and on the completion of his secondary
studies had gone on to the Madrid School of Fine Arts. Here his unconventional ideas on art and his sometimes erratic behavior irritated school authorities who, when they could take it no longer, suspended him. When, after
readmitting him, they found him just as untamed as before, he was permanently barred from further study. The professors and even the students shook
their heads over Dali. He was a wild one, they thought, perhaps actually mad.
And doubtless he was. His father had lavished money and attention on his

only son, and Salvador had lost his mother who might have given him greater stability. His father had hoped that his son would take over his office of notary "when he grew up," but it became more and more apparent that this would not come about. Dali was going to be a painter and that was that. Slowly his father began to turn against him.

In 1929 Dali went to Paris at the urging of friends who saw his work as potentially, or even actually, surrealist in character. They were right. Breton looked at his paintings and Dali was received with open arms, introduced to other members of the band and greatly encouraged to develop his art. This was a great shot in the arm for Dali, to know that his work was really appreciated after all the scorn that had been heaped upon it in the School of Fine Arts in Madrid. Of course he sold only a few paintings and even then at modest prices, but it was a beginning. When summer came, in 1930, he returned to Cadaques and invited many of his Paris friends to visit him there. Among the first were Paul Eluard and his wife, Elena, known as Gala by all her friends. She was a Russian émigré, a beautiful woman with reddish hair and a lively and forceful personality. Gala had decided ideas about life and art and how to handle men. She could be loving sometimes and frightening on other occasions. She was a close friend of most of the surrealists and they considered her their "Queen." She dressed beautifully because she had great taste and because Paul Eluard was one of the few among the surrealists who had a considerable income by inheritance. When she and Dali met in Cadaques, it was instant love, a deep, satisfying passion which has lasted through the years. She gave up her money, her comfort and devoted herself with a total oneness to the almost penniless Dali. This "oneness" was symbolized by Dali's insistance on signing his paintings "Dali and Gala." Eluard returned to Paris alone.

Needless to say, Salvador's father did not look upon this union with favor, and he let his feelings be known to the inhabitants of Cadaques. As a result no one would rent Salvador a room, many would not speak to him, but finally an older woman, the widow of a fisherman who lived over the hill to the north about a mile from the town, took pity on him. She resided in a minute fishing village where the fishermen lived with their wives in one-room houses huddled together at the edge of the bay of Port Lligat. Her name was Lidia Sabana de Costa and her occupation was mending the nets of the fishermen of the little village. I watched her day after day leaning over the nets, and when Dali approached her eyes would light up, and she would smile warmly. She owned two of the little houses on the port, and she allowed Dali to have one of them in the summertime free of charge. It was close quarters for two persons, especially since Dali used it for a studio also. It had only one window, in the front next to the door, which of course was open most of the time. At the back was a bed. In the front were a table and two chairs, a small stove for cooking, a few dishes and that was all. There was no running water, but plenty at the community pump in a nearby courtyard. If Dali had been "wild" before 1930, he showed no signs of it when I first met him three years later. At that time

The mysterious, attractive Elena ("Gala") Dali, Cadaques, Spain, 1933 *(Photo from the collection of Morrill Cody).*

Dali did not have the upturned, waxed mustache which he later affected and by which he is now internationally known. He was in fact rather reserved and rarely very communicative. He was absorbed by his painting and by nature and of course by Gala. He was adored by the village fishermen who brought him fish to eat and oddities of the sea, such as peculiar shells or unusual rocks, and when they talked with him you could see the love that shone in their eyes.

The summer I spent with them and the others I learned that Gala and Dali had a fixed schedule from which they almost never deviated. They rose with the dawn at four in the morning, and Dali painted until about seven. They must never be disturbed during those hours, I was told. Meanwhile the rest of us had gone at different times to the little pebble beach, which was another half mile or so beyond Port Lligat. This coast was so isolated, so completely devoid of human habitation in those days that we never saw anyone, not even fishermen in the bay. We felt the little beach belonged to us. Some have called this coast "desolate," but none of us thought so then or later. True, it had little vegetation except small patches of grass, an occasional cypress, and, where they had been planted many flourishing olive trees. The mountains, foothills of the Pyrenees, rose almost from the water to give a dramatic backdrop to the shining bays. So many of Dali's paintings include seascapes of the bay of Port Lligat, usually as a background. In fact, his paintings have so often contained his three obsessions: a portrait of Gala, the seascape, and a figure of a man with a little boy, the latter, Dali said, being his father and himself as a child. Mary and Marcel and Man Ray were so enchanted by the beauty of this coast that they returned many times for summer vacations in later years. I built a house there, a summer holiday spot at the farther end of Port Lligat bay.

At eleven, Dali and Gala would join the rest of us on the beach, where we would swim, sunbathe, and eventually eat the lunches we had brought with us. Dali wandered around the rocks along the coast, carrying a little hammer with which he would knock off some unusual rock formation, sometimes a thin lattice work of stone that had been beaten out by the lashing waves during winter storms. He would use these designs in his painting.

Gala said she wanted to learn to swim, and I agreed to teach her, but when I tried, she paid no attention to my instructions. Instead, she wanted me to take her out to the deeper water and bob around there in the buoyant water. So I would "tow" her out, and she would "stand" in the water, never sinking as long as she controlled her breathing. She was totally unafraid of water as long as I was not too far away. After a half hour or so, I would tow her back to shore. We did this every day, and while we bobbed around in the open water, we had long talks about her life, her ideals, and her hopes for the future. She was a fascinating woman. Years later she told me she had never learned to swim.

Talking was the best thing we did that summer. Day after day we sat on the beach exploring each other's minds and feelings, that is, all of us except Dali, who even deserted Gala to wander off by himself with his little hammer.

One day we were astonished to see six young girls, probably in their late teens or early twenties, come trooping over the hill accompanied by a matronly duenna. The girls turned out to be a mixture of English and Americans. The duenna was French. They all sat in a row in their prim dresses on the beach and stared at us. We were rather indignant at this invasion of our privacy and slightly embarrassed by the solemn curiosity of the girls; for all of us except Marcel and Mary were in the nude, our habitual costume for swimming. Marcel was dressed because he never went swimming, and Mary was in a bathing suit because, as she explained, she had a birthmark on her breast which she did not care to exhibit.

Then, after a few minutes, at a signal from the duenna, the six girls rose to their feet and quickly took off all their clothes and filed by us into the water. We soon followed them in, and the sight of eleven young people splashing around in the water, laughing and shouting, would have made a fine composition for an impressionist painting, or for a color photograph. When we came out we lent the girls towels to dry themselves before dressing again and returning over the hill as demurely as they had arrived. They were returning to Paris that afternoon, and we never saw them again.

As the afternoons waned we would gather up our own things and take the path back to Port Lligat, where we sometimes stopped to look at Dali's paintings and sketches. These were very productive years for him, and I believe that much of the credit for bringing this about was due to the loving strength he received from Gala who organized his life so painlessly. Once back at their little house Dali might paint some more, or sketch out ideas he had developed during the day or talk to the fishermen who by that time were often bringing in their catch. He almost never went into the town of Cadaques for fear of meeting his father, but he did see his sister, Anna Maria, occasionally at the little chapel, halfway into town. She too was devoted to him and, I believe, brought him food and money from time to time without his father's knowing about it.

We all marveled at Dali's genius in the technique of painting. He could, for instance, shift from painting a miniature of a few square inches to a full-sized canvas without a moment's hesitation. The little house was crowded with canvases and drawings, some of them mere sketches which he would develop when he returned to his larger studio in Paris.

In the evenings, Dali and Gala had a simple meal of fish and vegetables and fruit and went to bed with the sundown. After leaving Port Lligat, the rest of us would wander back to Cadaques where I often played chess with Marcel for an hour or two in one of the two local cafés. I was a mere novice at the game, and Marcel was an expert, but he played with me *faute de mieux*. Man Ray did not play chess in those days, but he took it up later and became one of Marcel's favorite opponents. Marcel had his own ideas about chess. One might call them surrealistic, or just plain unorthodox. After learning so much from him, I later tried his method out on orthodox players in New York, and they were horrified, indignant, outraged. "Of course you win when you play chess in that asinine way," they exclaimed.

On two occasions that summer, we rented a motorboat to take us to the farther point of land which faced across a big bay to France on the other side. This point of land had magnificent rock formations sculptured by the sea into easily imagined forms of animals, human figures, or designs of fantastic intricacy and beauty. We spent long hours looking at this remarkable natural wonderland. It is still there today, I am told.

At the end of the summer all of us except Gala and Dali went to Barcelona for a few days before returning to Paris. There we called on Picasso, who often spent his summers in Catalonia. I had never met him before. We sat with him in his studio over a glass of wine, and Marcel and Mary, who knew him best, told him of our summer in Cadaques. He had been invited there, too, but had been unable to make it, he said, because he had so much work to do. During this conservation, Picasso said, "I think Dali has more promise of becoming the greatest master of this century than any other painter I know." I often wondered in later life if he thought Dali fulfilled that promise.

Gala and Dali also returned to Paris two weeks later, and we all met again at his studio and at Mary's lovely house. One evening Gala took me aside to ask me if I would translate some writing of Dali's from French into English. I said I would, but I did not realize at first what a job I was taking on.

Dali had for some time been endeavoring to put on paper his ideas of painting, the mystical background of his personality, his fears and his hopes, all expressed in psuedo-Freudian terms, surrealist expressions, highly complex thoughts. I was baffled because I did not understand the real meaning of the words he wrote. When I appealed to Marcel for an explanation, I found he was no better informed than I. So I went ahead with a literal translation and hoped that some readers would understand what Dali was saying. This effort took me a couple of weeks, for there were pages and pages of it. When I finished I took it to Dali. He was delighted. He felt that he now had something he might show those Americans who admired his paintings and were constantly asking him just why he had painted this or that.

"I cannot pay you for your work," he said to me, "but I would like you to pick out one of my paintings or drawings as a payment for your work." I was delighted with his idea. I knew at once what I wanted, given such a free hand. It was a picture of Gala in a window with a "soft watch" draped over the window sill.

"Why did you pick that one?" he asked. "That is the only picture in the whole studio that I might sell. Julien Levy said he might give me fifty dollars for it and I said I would hold it for him until his return from New York next month. Take something else, anything. Of course Levy may not want that picture when he sees it again. In fact I will be greatly surprised if he does take it."

"If he doesn't, may I then have it?"

"Certainly."

"I'll wait," I said. As a result I never got any picture at all. In later years Dali remembered that I had made the first translations of his ideas into English, but he did not remember that he had promised me a painting. By that time his paintings were so valuable in monetary terms that I did not have the courage to remind him of his promise. The last time I saw the painting it was hanging in the Museum of Modern Art in New York.

Natalie Clifford Barney

NATALIE Clifford Barney was one of the rare people in this world. She got out of life about everything she wanted. Perhaps, if we can trust Ezra Pound's observation, she got even more. Pound admired Miss Barney for two things: *Pensées d'une Amazone*, her book of unfinished sentences and broken paragraphs; and a single sublime sentence that began, he remembered, " 'having got out of life perhaps more than it contains.' " Her aim was undoubtedly to enjoy her stay on this earth to the very limit of the objectives she had established for herself at an early age. While still in her early twenties she knew that above all she wished to live in Paris, to know many people in the world of literature, and to lead a life peculiar to herself without disapproving interference from outsiders. She liked and admired both men and women for their intelligence and their cultural achievements; but for the passionate emotional experiences she longed for, she knew that she must turn to women only. She never wavered from these desires and she carried them off with courage and social grace.

Natalie was born in Dayton, Ohio, in 1877, into a family whose ancestors included judges, bank presidents, and naval heroes. Her mother, Alice Barney, achieved a considerable reputation as a society portrait painter. Natalie and her sister, Laura, only children, were educated by governesses, and both received a fine education with an overlay of European culture. At twenty-five Natalie was a beautiful young woman with shiny brown hair, a rosy face, steel blue eyes, and a fine, graceful figure. She also had remarkable poise and self-assurance without being forward.

Before moving to France, she visited Mytilene (ancient Lesbos), in the

Natalie Clifford Barney (right) with her sister, Laura. Paris, 1915 (*Photo courtesy of George Wickes*).

company of Renée Vivien, a turn-of-the-century poetess of legendary beauty and accomplishment. The two women proposed to found a colony of women poets in honor of Sappho, but when their plan did not materialize Natalie decided to settle in Paris. In 1909, after a brief residence in Neuilly, on the outskirts of the city, she rented a sixteenth-century house with a beautiful garden at number 20 rue Jacob, a narrow little street that runs parallel to the Seine between the river and St. Germain des Prés. Natalie's house, still standing, has four floors and displays some fine ironwork on the little window balconies. Behind it is a considerable garden with a small temple with Doric columns in the style of the First Empire. Chiseled over the entrance in stone are the words: "A l'Amitié." By Natalie's friends it was always called the Temple of Friendship. Today, this little edifice is classified as a national monument. It may never be destroyed or moved away without government permission.

At 20 rue Jacob, Natalie lived for more than sixty years. There she died in 1972, at the age of ninety-five.

Among her close friends in the early years was Remy de Gourmont, the noted literary critic, who lived nearby. French literary historians, incorrigibly

Natalie Clifford Barney, a fashionable young lady in Paris, about 1910 *(Photo courtesy of George Wickes).*

romantic, credit Natalie with being Gourmont's "inspiration." The admiring English writer Richard Aldington wrote that it was Miss Barney who "startled this disfigured old recluse out of his dusty books, and restored him to life." Be that as it may, she was certainly his strong financial supporter in the years when living by the pen became difficult for him. In gratitude, he addressed to her a volume entitled *Lettres à l'Amazone*. And it was as the "Amazone" that she was henceforth to be known.

But de Gourmont was only the most famous of many men and women whom Natalie helped financially when the need arose. She was generous, and she asked nothing in return.

Natalie was thirty-two when she established herself in the rue Jacob, and from that time on, except during the war years, she entertained lavishly but not ostentatiously all the literary people—French, American, and English—who cared to come to her Temple of Friendship. Unlike Gertrude Stein she shunned tourists and curiosity seekers. She gave no interviews, refused all inquiries about her parties. It was primarily because of this insistence on secrecy that her parties took on a greater significance than they really deserved. Wittingly or not, she created a legend about her person which never

Natalie Clifford Barney, in Paris, about 1910 *(Photo courtesy of George Wickes).*

ceased to grow. Just who came to her parties is not really known, but it is known who her "regulars" were, those she counted on to make her salon attractive. She prided herself on the international character of her salon and tried to mix a variety of people who would not ordinarily meet. In the twenties she introduced American and English writers to the French. At one time or another, Cocteau, Pound, Ford, Gertrude Stein, Fitzgerald, Sherwood Anderson, Colette, France, Gide, Rilke, and Valéry all enjoyed her exotic surroundings and cuisine. Although Natalie preferred writers to composers, she entertained Darius Milhaud and Florent Schmitt, and permitted Pound and his protégé George Antheil to perform their music in her salon.

I can well believe all the stories about her salon from seeing the notables at the two Friday evening gatherings I attended. There were many others there, too, nonnotables, but often very interesting people, and especially outstanding were some very handsome women. Sometimes those evenings included readings, music, or other entertainment. Always, champagne and cocktails flowed

Inside the Temple of Friendship *(Photo courtesy of George Wickes).*

generously; the hors d'oeuvres, irresistible, were prepared by a noted caterer and served by a butler with a bald pate, lacquered, on which he had painted a neat head of hair—all in nice French curlicues.

Guests were there by invitation, but it was understood that an invited guest could bring one or two friends who were not yet on the invitation list, a not unusual procedure at literary salons, a few of which still exist in Paris today.

But Natalie's life was not merely filled with parties and love affairs, as some have reported. She also wrote poetry, mostly in French, some of which she published in private editions. She studied music, read all the new literature, and maintained a high intellectual level for discussions with her gifted friends. Altogether, she was a remarkable woman with a divine gift for making others happy, especially women.

Two women she made happy were Radclyffe Hall and Djuna Barnes, both lesbians, both writers. Sylvia Beach regretted not meeting Radclyffe Hall at Natalie's salon, but recalled that the author had said in her controversial novel about lesbianism, *The Well of Loneliness,* that "inverted couples" would have fewer, if any, problems if they could be "united at the altar." That was a conclusion that Natalie would no doubt emphatically reject, and as Valérie Seymour in Miss Hall's novel, she was allowed to do so. In casting her friend

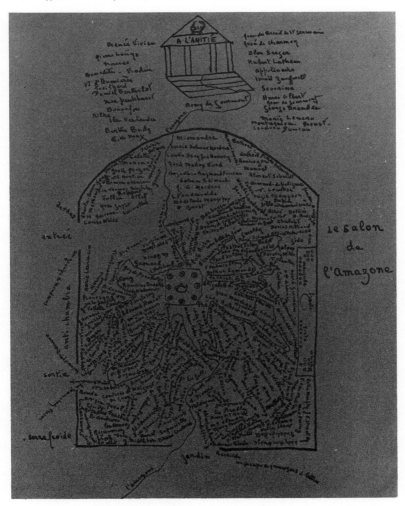

Map and table of contents (drawn by André Rouveyre), listing the names of the people who visited Natalie's salon. The floor plan shows a tea table with eight place settings (middle) and sideboard (right) with drinks. At the top is the Temple of Friendship *(Photo courtesy of George Wickes).*

Natalie as the fictional character Valérie Seymour, Radclyffe Hall intended to present a lesbian who rises above the suffering and anquish experienced by other lesbians in the novel. The difference between Valérie and the others was the acceptance of lesbianism: she came to terms with it, the others did not. Djuna Barnes, on the other hand, presented similar material in her *Ladies Almanack,* but treated it satirically rather than tragically. She poked fun at the well-known lesbians in Paris, singling out particularly a character she called Evangeline Musset, a patron saint of lesbians, whose pontifical manner and apostolic zeal she ridiculed. That she had Natalie in mind—the "pope of the

"The Lady (Natalie Clifford Barney) and her page," a scene from one of Natalie's masquerades *(Photo courtesy of George Wickes).*

lesbos" Claude Mauriac called her—there is no reason to doubt. Even Radclyffe Hall had Valérie Seymour say in a scene set in a homosexual bar: "I think I preferred it when we were all martyrs."

In the later years of her life, Natalie's circle of friends and her activities became more restricted, but the quality of her gatherings, I am told, never diminished. When she was already in her nineties, the owner of her house made signs of wanting to disposses her in order to convert it into apartments. When this reached the newspapers, there were loud protests from influential French intellectuals. One of the owners of the property was Jacques Chaban Delmos, the president of the National Assembly and a former prime minister

Natalie Clifford Barney (right) with Djuna Barnes, novelist and poet, author of *Ladies Almanack* and *Nightwood*. Beauvallon, 1927 *(Photo courtesy of George Wickes)*.

Natalie Clifford Barney (right) with Romaine Brooks, American painter and longtime friend, in Florence, 1945 *(Photo courtesy of George Wickes)*.

of France. As soon as he heard of it, he intervened and announced that as long as Miss Barney lived, she would never lose her home in the rue Jacob. Natalie Barney remains a revered literary figure, but more in France than in America.

Isadora Duncan

OF all the women of Montparnasse, Isadora Duncan was without doubt the most romantic, idealistic, expressive of her love, persistent in her aims, unabashed in her desires and at the same time the most impractical in many ways, but not in others. She was improvident, overly generous with most people, and grasping with others. She was also a beautiful girl and woman, an extraordinarily graceful dancer, and a potent force in the liberalization of the dance from the traditional discipline which had marked it for a hundred years previously. She introduced a whole new concept to the dance, and the leaders of that art today have followed in her footsteps. Isadora captivated most men and some women, she shocked and alienated many others because of what they termed her "immorality." She believed in free love, free political expression, justice for the underdog, and manna for the creative artists. She was utterly inconsistent, for despite her agonies for the poor and the needy, she loved luxury for herself. Many would call her wanton, selfish, a seeker of publicity, a saint, a goddess, an extraordinary dancer of graceful rhythmic beauty.

Isadora was not exactly a product of Montparnasse, for she came to live there only toward the end of her life when her greatest days were past. It was at that time—she was well into her forties—that I knew her. She lived in a studio that faced the back door of the Dôme café on the Rue Delambre. Here almost nightly many people gathered to talk, to drink, and, after the crowd had dwindled, to see Isadora dance her rhythms of Chopin, Beethoven, Wagner, and Liszt, an inspiring sight despite any reservations one might have about the character of her life. Everyone was invited, but the guests were expected to bring with them wine or cognac or Pernod, but especially champagne, for

Isadora Duncan, wearing a Grecian-styled tunic, dancing in the Amphitheatre of Dionysius, Athens, 1904 *(Photo from the Dance Collection, The New York Public Library at Lincoln Center, Astor, Lenox and Tilden Foundations).*

Isadora drank only that. To these parties came the rich, the important, the intellectuals, students, artists, models, writers, members of the press, and simply admirers of all ages and nationalities. Many did not stay, others lingered until the small hours. Isadora received all with open arms, even when she obviously did not know them. She always danced in her bare feet, and her costume was so meager that she was nearly nude.

Isadora had a style of conversation that was both emotional and intelligent. She was best at this in the afternoon, before the guests of the evening arrived, when I could sit with her alone for an hour or so. She would talk about her views on how to right the injustices of the world, reform political prejudices, bring happiness to the downtrodden. Much that she said was practical, and much was idealistic rubbish.

Although I enjoyed being with Isadora, I was afraid of her. I did not want to become involved with her. If I went too far, she would "eat me up," I feared, just as she had done to so many other men. Some other men I knew had this same fear. I had no desire to try to tame her. Certainly there was much that was appealing in her, much that was the little girl still.

La Duncan began life in San Francisco in 1877 and, as a small child, had naturally learned to express herself in the dance. She tried a few lessons in a ballet school, but found that distasteful and soon gave it up in favor of a rhythmic self-expression of her own composition. Her scorn for ballet lasted through her entire life. She called it "gymnastics." Aided by her mother, a piano teacher, and her sister, Elizabeth, and two brothers, Augustine and Raymond, she endeavored to arouse interest in her special type of dance, but without much success in the early years. Yet she persisted, moving with the whole family from the West to Chicago and then to New York and on to Europe, where she finally found in Germany the recognition she desired. Success when it came was tremendous—in Berlin, in Hungary, in Vienna, in Paris, in Italy, and in Russia.

It was a magic world of flaming enthusiasm and adulation and joy. She had a tremendous capacity for joy, unrestrained and uninhibited. She also had a tremendous capacity for sorrow and despair that sometimes brought her to the verge of suicide. There was in her life no time for quiet, sensible normality. She had to be at the top or the bottom, but in either case it had to be a highly charged emotional state. She and her family began to build a stone temple in Greece, and she invested all the money she had made from successful dance tours in its construction. It was to be their spiritual home. It was only when they had completed the foundations that they discovered there was no water there, or even within a couple of miles of their property. Raymond started to dig a well, but he never found any water either. At the same time Isadora and her sister endeavored to found an all-boy Greek chorus on the order of the ancient Hellenic style, but she soon discovered that little Greek boys were just as difficult to handle as little American boys.

Isadora wanted above all to establish a school for children who would grow up with the knowledge and enthusiasm to carry on her art of the dance when she was gone. She began several times in this direction and on more than one occasion with ample financial backing, but in each case something interfered with the project—a new love affair, a desire to move her headquarters, or sometimes a too lavish expenditure of her capital. Only in Greece did she get important financial help from the government, but a political upset forced her to leave the country at the moment that things were getting under way, and just as she seemed on the verge of success.

Among her many lovers was Gordon Craig, the noted stage designer and son of England's greatest actress, Ellen Terry. But this went on the rocks when he

Isadora Duncan with her children, Deirdre (5) and Patrick (3, whose father was Paris Singer), 1912 *(Photo from the Dance Collection, The New York Public Library at Lincoln Center, Astor, Lenox and Tilden Foundations).*

wanted her to give up her dancing, marry him, and "settle down" to being his dutiful wife in a conventional atmosphere. His disdain of her "art" was the final blow. "I will never marry," Isadora proclaimed. "I saw what marriage did to my mother. It is a barbarous custom which kills love and joy." Later, for the same reason, she gave up her violent attachment to Paris Singer, the sewing-machine heir, who also wanted her to marry him and "enjoy his money for the rest of her life." She enjoyed his money, with which he was more than generous to her, especially in trying to help her found her long-sought school of the dance, but jealousy and temperament intervened, though they maintained a now-and-then liaison for quite a few years.

Meanwhile, she continued to make dance tours in many cities of the world,

Isadora Duncan and stage designer Gordon Craig, the day they met in Berlin, 1904. Craig was the father of Isadora's first child *(Photo from the Dance Collection, The New York Public Library at Lincoln Center, Astor, Lenox and Tilden Foundations).*

including those of the United States where, with Walter Damrosch and his great symphony orchestra, she enthralled audiences everywhere. Occasionally, she was forced to dance to music played by less-qualified orchestras, and in such cases the audience might not react with its usual enthusiasm. This she blamed on the poor quality of the music, and she was undoubtedly right.

Then in the twenties she was invited to the Soviet Union, where she was told she would be given all facilities to found her long-desired school of the dance. When she got there she found that the Soviets had a different idea of the life style of a famous dancer other than their own. Despite being somewhat disenchanted, she conceived of the Soviet Union as the promise of Utopia because she was moved by its goals and its sufferings and because its government subsidized art. "I am red, red," she exclaimed, "a revolutionary," while at the same time denying she was a Bolshevik. Like many others her politics were emotional, not in any way political. She fell in love with a wild young poet named Serge Esenin, fifteen years her junior. Then she decided that she must get out of Russia, but this, she found, was impossible if she wished to take Serge with her. The only solution to the problem was to marry him.

What a pair they made. She spoke no Russian, and he spoke nothing else. Their only communication was love with a capital L. Another small problem in their lives was the fact that he was mad, actually insane, and finally he was locked up in an asylum. He broke up furniture, insulted everyone in sight, put on horrible scenes of jealousy. He was particularly offensive to American

Isadora Duncan and the Russian poet Sergei Esenin, Berlin, May 1922, the month they married *(Photo from the Dance Collection, The New York Public Library at Lincoln Center, Astor, Lenox and Tilden Foundations).*

audiences. In America, where Isadora had unwisely taken him on tour, not only was he offensive and utterly rude to those he encountered, but she, too, decided to make a one-woman campaign to tell the Americans how brutishly unjust they had been to Sacco and Vanzetti and how this immoral execution could never have happened in that great bastion of liberty, the Soviet Union. Her American tour was a disaster. When she left, she vowed never to return to America, and she never did.

Back in Europe, Serge longed for a country where he knew the language, where she would be his wife and not a theatrical star. And so Isadora sent him home to Moscow in the company of her maid, where he was promptly put under the control that he obviously needed. Isadora remained in Paris, and when she was asked why her husband had gone back to Russia, she explained that he would be better off there. The Russians loved him even if he was foolish. And there he could smash things up and no one would care "because he is a poet." A little over two years later however, aged only thirty, he hanged himself in room number 5 in the Hotel Angleterre in Leningrad.

Once again Isadora was left alone. She had borne two children, one by Gordon Craig and one by Paris Singer, but both had drowned in an accident in the Seine. Her mother and sister and one brother had returned to the United

Isadora Duncan, Paris, 1920s *(Photo from Princeton Theatre Collection, Princeton University).*

States, and her brother Raymond had established himself on the Left Bank and in Neuilly with a group of followers of the ancient Greek traditions. Her dance tours continued, but she was no longer the beautiful, young, lithe creature she had been in her youth. She still danced remarkably well, but it was not quite the same. Some younger women were imitating her style. It was in this period that I knew her and liked her enthusiasm and vitality. It was in this period, too, that she wrote her incredibly frank memoirs, finishing the work in the early summer of 1927.

One day in September 1927, she was in Nice and had persuaded the local Bugatti dealer to give her a trial ride in one of their sports models. She loved fast motorcars. Around her neck she wore a long red scarf. It was, she said, the symbol of her rebellion against injustice in the world. Just as she left on her fatal auto drive she exclaimed, "Goodbye, friends. I am going to glory." As the car sped down the road the scarf became entangled in the rear wheel and in an instant it tightened around her neck and in a thousandth of a second she was dead. It was a dramatic end to a great dancer and to one of the most romantic women of her era.

Margaret Anderson

I first met Margaret Anderson in 1916, I believe, when I was only fifteen, but my mother had known her for two or three years before that. She moved into a house a few doors from us in Lake Bluff, Illinois, a small town of five or six hundred, thirty miles north of Chicago. She didn't have any time to waste on a high school boy, but I didn't want to *talk* to her. I just wanted to look at her, for I thought she was the most beautiful woman I had ever seen, with her golden blond hair that shone like a halo around her head. I also enjoyed her music. She was a gifted amateur pianist, especially with the works of Chopin. She could have been professional if she had wished to devote her energies in that direction. She had a fine figure and wore her "uniform" with tremendous style. We called it a uniform because she never wore anything else: a tailored suit so deep a blue that some thought it was black, a white blouse open at the neck, and a little dark blue hat on the top of her head. Winter or summer she never wore anything else. She said they were the only clothes she had except a dressing gown and a bathing suit.

For anyone interested in literature, and especially in poetry, Chicago was an exciting place to be in those years. It became a lively but temporary collecting point for many young writers devoted to new ways of self-expression, new art forms, new depths of meaning. Eventually they moved on to Montparnasse by way of New York. In Chicago, in 1912, Harriet Monroe founded *Poetry, A Magazine of Verse*, in which such giants-to-be as Carl Sandburg, Vachel Lindsay, and Edgar Lee Masters were happy to see their poetry appear. Harriet Monroe had a fine sensitivity to what was important in this new expression, and she presented it to the interested public in a manner worthy of its importance.

An elegant Margaret Anderson, southern France, 1926 *(Photo courtesy of the Library of Congress).*

Lake Bluff, where my parents lived, played a small role in all this because of the presence of Alice Corbin, a poet and assistant editor of *Poetry*. She and her painter husband, William Penhallow Henderson, lived right across the street from us, and she and my mother were devoted friends. They also had a daughter whom Eunice Tietjens, another subeditor of *Poetry*, called that "uncontrolled child." Since her name was also Alice, she was usually referred to as "little Alice" and her mother as "big Alice." "Little Alice" and I were also devoted friends.

The Henderson property extended toward Lake Michigan, and on this big lot stood twenty cabins, known as the "little tin cottages" because of their corrugated tin roofs. Each cottage had a small bedroom, sufficient for one person or a very loving couple, and a living-room–dining-room–kitchen combination with a table and several straight chairs. The facilities were primitive to say the least, but people were used to such inconveniences in those days. And the compensation came with the rent, only five dollars a month. There was usually a waiting list for these cottages in the summer, but "big Alice" always gave preference to writers and artists. Quite a colony gathered there every year, including Vachel Lindsay, Edgar Lee Masters, and William Vaughn Moody. Masters was particularly nice to "little Alice" and me, for he had a warm heart for children. Sandburg did not visit Lake Bluff, as far as I know, and years later I asked him why. "I didn't have the time. I was very busy," he said, but I have an idea that he and Masters had a little jealousy between them, and Carl did not wish to "invade" Masters's territory. Eunice Tietjens was also a frequent visitor, as were many luminaries of the Chicago literary scene. Of course, Harriet Monroe came out, too. She was a severe woman in outward aspect, but she had a warm and understanding heart.

The second magazine to appear in Chicago was the *Little Review*. The founder and editor Margaret Anderson, was a twenty-three-year-old woman of little literary education and almost no experience in magazine publishing. She was, however, a fountain of exuberant enthusiasm. Eunice Tietjens, who was present at the gathering in the spring of 1914 when the magazine was founded, describes her as an "incredible mixture of adolescent dreams and vitality of colossal blindness, and of a kind of savage scorn of everything she did not understand." Margaret Anderson's enthusiasm was like a tidal wave that swept all before it, irresistible, engulfing, yet joyous and exhilarating. Everyone felt Margaret's dynamic presence. Mostly it induced intense admiration and love, but sometimes distate, envy, irritation, and even fear. Her feelings were rare, however. One gift that no one disputed was her almost infallible sense of what was important in literature, and when she found an example, as she did with Joyce's *Ulysses* a few years later, she stayed with it through thick and thin.

The first number of the *Little Review* contained all the faults that one might expect. It was badly edited, badly printed. "I did not know," she explained, "that you had to read proofs after they came from the printer." Reading proofs was a bore. Margaret had no sense of discipline or any sense of the art of publishing, unlike Harriet Monroe, who turned *Poetry* into a model of the printing and editorial arts. Her practice was to sweep all these small matters aside and with them any criticism of the magazine. All would be improved in the next issue, she promised—if there was a next issue. There always was, somehow, by miracles she never explained. Margaret had no money, no place to live, and a complete and total confidence that someone would provide. A young man who could ill afford the expense financed the first two issues, and after he dropped out, many others came along to fill the gap. Eunice Tietjens gave Margaret her diamond engagement ring to sell to pay for one issue of the magazine.

As for the literary and artistic content of the *Little Review*, it was a hodgepodge of scraps of this and that, many written by Margaret herself. Early contributors were mostly Chicagoans—Floyd Dell, Vachel Lindsay, Sara Teasdale, Eunice Tietjens, Maxwell Bodenheim, Amy Lowell, Witter Bynner, and Conrad Aiken. The list was long and the magazine worth subscribing to if one was willing to hunt for the best pieces. Margaret could not afford to pay a

Margaret Anderson (right, in white dress) with Georgette Leblanc and the young American composer George Antheil, Bernardsville, New Jersey, 1920 (*Photo courtesy of Allen Tanner*).

cent for the material she printed. Contributors were simply expected to share her electric enthusiasm for the *Little Review*. Despite its weaknesses, Margaret's magazine struck a new note which a small but fervent readership would carry to an international level.

Gradually, new authors like Sherwood Anderson and Ben Hecht heard about the *Little Review*, and the quality of the contents rose markedly. It was in this period that Margaret and her "staff" came to live briefly in Lake Bluff. The "staff" consisted of Margaret's sister, Lois, with her two children, her editorial helper Harriet Dean, and the invaluable Clara, who cooked and shopped when there was any money or credit available, and her little son who clogged beautifully. Others came and went. Since none had any regular source of income, they sometimes went hungry. My mother and I saw them almost daily, and I think it was she who hinted that occasional groceries might be charged to my father's account at the only grocery store in town. Margaret did not have to be urged. Before nightfall a big supply of canned goods, meat, vegetables, and fruit found its way to the Anderson ménage. When my father found out what was happening a week later, he immediately put a stop to it. Although a writer himself, he had no sympathy with "flighty young women magazine editors." He and Margaret had words that everyone could hear. He did pay for the groceries already delivered, however, mostly because he had no choice, and thus he too, however grudgingly, became an important contributor to another issue of the *Little Review*. But from that time on the Cody relationship with the editorial staff was strained, to say the least. I was forbidden to see them, but I went anyway when my father was not around. I believe my mother did also. Anyway, Margaret had in one week acquired enough food to keep the band going for a little while longer. But a few months later, far behind in the rent, they moved "by request," this time to some tents on the Lake Michigan beach near Ravinia Park where the rent was free.

By the end of the summer most of Margaret's "staff" had deserted her. They decided the rigors of beach life were beyond their endurance. Only Harriet Dean remained faithful to the end when they finally moved back to Chicago. It was now 1917, and this was to be the beginning of the *Little Review's* greatest success. First, Margaret acquired Jane Heap as her principal editorial assistant. A talented young woman of Norwegian origin, Jane was a deep and orderly thinker, a skillful but sluggish writer, a pertinacious critic, and a born editor. She provided intellectual ballast and emotional balance. She was a brilliant talker. It was Jane who gave the *Little Review* a quotable working formula: "To express the emotions of life is to live. To express the life of the emotions is to make art." Aphoristic proclamations like these prompted floods of superlatives from Margaret. "To me the expression, the formulation, of Jane's thoughts amounted to genius." Margaret herself had no pretensions to knowing the things about life and art that Jane knew and articulated; so she cast herself as an appreciator and demander, hounding her friend, whom she called the creator, to convert her nimble, piercing, and intelligent talk into writing, and hence into the permanent record of the *Little Review*. Margaret's entreaties were effective. Jane once commented, "You pushed me into the arena, and I performed to keep you quiet."

Another noted addition to the staff was Ezra Pound. From England, he wrote the editors telling them of Eliot, Joyce, Wyndham Lewis, Ford, and Yeats. In May 1917 Margaret appointed him foreign editor, thus guaranteeing that the *Little Review* would become a place where he, with the others, could appear regularly. With Pound's infusion, the *Little Review* grew from a dull and somewhat pretentious publication into a formidable dispenser of the new literature. Pound was as delighted as the editors with the transformation, but Margaret always stoutly denied that she and Jane were unduly influenced by their man in London. Pound had sent *Ulysses*, of course, but he had not influenced her to publish it. No, she did that because she had loved *A Portrait of the Artist as a Young Man* and because the opening chapters of *Ulysses* contained such "magic words."

MARGARET ANDERSON

Photograph by Victor Georg

jh

Photograph by E. O. Hoppé

EDITORS OF THE LITTLE REVIEW

A page from the *Little Review*, Vol 9, No. 2, Margaret Anderson and Jane Heap, editors of the *Little Review*, 1918.

After a brief interlude in California, Margaret moved her magazine to New York, where she and Jane continued to lead the same hand-to-mouth existence, although they fared considerably better because sponsors and financial contributors were numerous there. In the March 1918 issue, Margaret began the serialization of a substantial portion of Joyce's controversial novel *Ulysses*.

When someone asked Margaret what critical standards guided her editorial decisions, hinting that maybe there weren't any standards at all, she replied: "*Mon dieu,*" did I have any standards? I had nothing *but!*" Margaret could be ornery; she could be an imperious arbiter of taste; her self-assurance could escalate to inflexibility. She continued: "I would accept only that writing which met, even in the slightest degree, my touchstone judgments." A touchstone to Margaret was the "kind of person who could prove that, in his case, the despised terms 'I like' or 'I don't like' were important, authentic, and *right*." For example, the morning *Ulysses* arrived, Margaret had been brought to the verge of tears when, rushing through the opening chapter, she had read, "Ineluctable modality of the visible." Jane shared Margaret's emotion, and they determined to publish it at once. "We were terribly moved; we kept saying, "What ART!" To a reader puzzled by Joyce's meaning, Margaret explained: "I don't think of what it means. . . . Joyce has produced a paragraph of great prose—in other words, ART." Margaret the touchstone was inviolable.

For three years *Little Review* subscribers grappled with excerpts from the great novel. At one point postal censors seized four issues of the magazine, charging that Joyce's book was obscene. It was Margaret's greatest triumph. When the Society for the Suppression of Vice finally brought Margaret into court for selling obscene material to a minor, she pleaded not guilty. The celebrated trial that followed, in which Joyce's friend and patron, John Quinn, defended the editor, ended in glorious defeat. Art never claimed a more regal and pugnacious martyr. Only the fine of one hundred dollars was a disappointment. Margaret hoped that she would be sent to jail.

And now, once again, Margaret was going through one of her restless desires for change. She particularly wanted to go to Europe, to see for herself what the intellectual life there had to offer her. She was not sure that she wished to continue struggling with the *Little Review*. It had started to bore her, though she still enjoyed the attention she received as its editor. Then one day a friend from Chicago, Allen Tanner, introduced her to Georgette Leblanc, the former wife of the dramatist and symbolist Maurice Maeterlinck, and a singer and diseuse of some repute. Drawn to each other immediately, they formed a union that remained unbroken until Georgette's death twenty-one years later.

Margaret was delighted when Georgette asked her to become her accompanist on a tour of Europe in 1924. Jane Heap went along, too, but stayed abroad only a short time, for she had decided to keep the magazine going on her own initiative in New York. From that time on Margaret Anderson no longer edited the *Little Review* herself, even though her name still appeared at the top of the masthead. She did continue, however, to collect material for Jane in Europe and to take a lively interest in the magazine's progress. Under Jane's direction, it soon became a quarterly and at times a semiannual by combining two issues into one. She also increased the number of translations by young French writers of the day, such as Paul Eluard and Jules Romains, whose works had never appeared in America before.

When Margaret reached Paris, she expected to find the same kind of opposition to her ideas that she had encountered in Chicago and New York, but to her surprise—and perhaps I should also say her dismay—no one tried to tell her what she might say or print. There was no moralistic hue and cry about anything. The only people she found to fight with were taxi drivers, concierges, and landlords, and with them she became very irritated when she found that battling against their stubbornness was futile. She displayed her dislike of the French even though she considered France her spiritual home. What she failed to realize was that the French themselves had been struggling against the French for centuries without any success. Her annoyance showed itself in many ways, and it tended to intimidate the important people she met, some of whom were contributors to the *Little Review*. They somehow felt that she who had recognized so early the new literary movements in Europe would be structured more like themselves, that she would discuss, not argue. But Margaret had been brought up on arguing and felt unhappy when a good verbal battle was hard to find. When she met Ezra Pound, with whom she had worked so successfully for many years, she could only remark, "It would be more interesting to know him when he was grown up."

Her comments on a few of the writers she met were astute, particularly her remark on meeting Hemingway. Reduced to one word, she said Hemingway is "simple." And indeed he was, just that, in the years before he began to create his own myth and surround himself with phobias and not-so-simple. As a simple man he had great charm, but this he lost after success overtook him.

When I met Margaret again, in 1924, she spoke warmly of my mother, and she remembered my father's "words" with her, but I found her less interesting than I had expected. She was so involved with her own special ideas and emotions that she had little patience for communication in other fields. And fortunately Margaret also began to realize that by being irritated with what she found in France, she alienated the very people she had come there to meet. She changed her approach, especially toward the French, but in the process she began to withdraw from the world of literature and art and to enter, along with Georgette Leblanc, a world of mysticism, soul searching philosophy, and emotional immersion.

For some time she and Georgette were members of the colony of women who studied with the Russo-Greek philosopher and mystic Gurdjieff at the Institute for the Harmonious Development of Man, at Fontainebleu-Avon, a village near Paris. With this analyst of thought and emotion also lived Katherine Mansfield until her death in 1923. Although Gurdjieff's messianic teachings often irritated Margaret to the point of outright disagreement with the master, she and Georgette remained under his sway long after they had left the institute.

Margaret Anderson, in repose, and Jane Heap, early 1920s *(Photo from the papers of Sylvia Beach, Princeton University Library).*

In 1929 Jane and Margaret finally decided to bring the *Little Review* to an end. The final issue, published in Paris, consisted largely of replies they had received to a questionnaire sent to their most important contributors and to certain friends who had helped with the magazine. The questions give a clue to the state of mind of both women, although Jane Heap's pessimism out-weighed Margaret's by a considerable margin. These were the questions:

What should you most like to do, to know, to be? Why wouldn't you change places with any other human being? What do you look forward to? What has been the happiest moment of your life? The unhappiest? What do you consider your weakest characteristics? Your strongest? What do you like most about yourself? Dislike most? What things do you really like? Dislike? What is your attitude toward art today? What is your worldview? Why do you go on living?

The questions of course reveal more about Margaret than about those who gamely tried to answer them. They are hardly questions one can answer honestly in print. But no dissembling disguised the editors' explanations why, after fifteen years, they had joined to inter the *Little Review*. Margaret first: "I can no longer go on publishing a magazine in which no one really knows what he is talking about." Jane followed:

For years, we offered the *Little Review* as a trial-track for racers. We hoped to find artists who could run with the great artists of the past . . . who could make new records. But you can't get race horses from mules. . . . We have given space . . . to twenty-three new systems of art (all now dead), representing 19 countries. In all of this we have not brought forward anything approaching a masterpiece except *Ulysses*.

But even a despondent Jane could not dim the *Little Review*'s imposing reputation as the place where so much of our enduring art first appeared. And for this we are indebted to Margaret the founder, appreciator and demander, who, shortly before her death, reiterated her indebtedness to Jane, the creator, this way: "If I could start a new *Little Review* today, I would be satisfied if I had only one contributor: Jane Heap."

After a few years in France, Margaret became more and more emotionally bound to the country, and especially to the old France of castles and art and to the poetry of the sea along her shores. She became increasingly attached to Georgette and to that "perfect companion," Monique, Georgette's faithful *dame de campaigne*, who remained with them both as long as she lived. A few other close friends were important, too, notably, Solita Solano, a critic and novelist, Janet Flanner, the Paris correspondent of the *New Yorker*, who wrote a very fine essay on Margaret when she died, and Dorothy Caruso, the widow of the great singer. But after 1929, the date of the last issue of the *Little Review*, Margaret faded from the literary and artistic scene in which she had played such a tremendous role. One wonders how she could have made such a complete change of character.

In 1941 Georgette Leblanc died in the tiny house they called the Chalet Rose, at Le Cannet, near Cannes. Shortly thereafter friends persuaded Margaret to return to the United States. On the boat home she met Dorothy Caruso, who was understanding and selfless, and another firm friendship was established. This, too, was broken only when Dorothy died in 1955. Margaret went back to France, back to Monique and the little house in Le Cannet where she lived for the rest of her life, even after Monique died in 1961. In 1957, when Sylvia Beach and I put on the 1920s exhibit at the American Cultural Center in Paris, I wrote to Margaret asking her to lend us any documents or photographs she might have pertaining to the *Little Review*. She replied at once and sent us some copies of the *Little Review* and some photographs. I also invited her to come to Paris for the opening with all her expenses paid, but she refused saying that she was not able to make the trip. I fear she had lost her taste for the limelight. She told me she was writing but could not find a publisher for her work.

Margaret lived to the age of eighty-two, always a free spirit, positive of her own ideas, devoted to emotional love, peace, and undying friendship for those she loved. I am not sure that she realized what an important role, along with Jane Heap and Ezra Pound, she had played in bringing so very many important writers and artists to the attention of the thinking public in America and elsewhere through the *Little Review*. It was a task that only Margaret Anderson, with her incredible drive and enthusiasms, could have carried on for fifteen years. What a triumph!

Janet Flanner, Berenice Abbott, and Florence Gilliam

A few women who made a deep and permanent mark on the social and artistic life of Paris in the twenties also left a vivid record of what happened there. Probably no more scintillating description of life in France, notably Paris, exists than that created by Janet Flanner in her fortnightly letters from Paris to the *New Yorker*, available today under the titles *Paris Journal* and *Paris Was Yesterday*. Like many of us in Paris at the time, Janet grew up in the American Midwest, a region, Ford Madox Ford used to say, that had produced nearly all the Americans he encountered in Paris. Janet was born in Indianapolis in 1892, attended the University of Chicago, and came to Paris in 1922 with Solita Solano, an American friend from Michigan with whom she had spent the previous year touring Europe and the Middle East. Paris, they had decided, was where they would write their first novels. They settled down in the Hotel Napoleon Bonaparte, close by the Seine, the Louvre, buses, and one block away from the cafés Deux Magots and the Flore. For their accommodations in what must have been the narrowest hotel in Paris—it measured only two rooms wide—they paid one dollar a day. They stayed nineteen years.

Whatever it may have lacked in amenities, their hotel more than made up for in what the two women wanted most: privacy, no domesticity, and the stimulating life of Montparnasse. It was indeed their ideal, an "all-purpose hotel." There they wrote their novels, quickly, gracefully, and successfully. Three by Solita—*The Uncertain Feast* (1924), *The Happy Failure* (1925), and *This Way Up* (1926)—and one by Janet, *The Cubical City* (1926), were all published by Putnam's. But after 1926 they never again wrote another. "Writing fiction," Janet said a few years ago, "is not my gift. Writing is but not

Janet Flanner, on the balcony of her room at the Ritz Hotel, Paris, 1972 *(Photo from the collection of Hugh Ford).*

writing fiction." Solita, who became an expert critic, completed a collection of poetry, however, *Statue in a Field*.

There were times when the two women found out that even a fifth floor roost didn't always guarantee total privacy. Once when Isadora Duncan discovered their hideaway, she waited outside the Napoleon for Janet in a rented car. Isadora's habit, recalled Solita, "was to invite people, any people, for drinks at cafés, then someone solid, a non-drinker, would have to be found who would be good for the final bill." Janet was caught once, but never again. Another time, Djuna Barnes, complaining of illness, slept in their quarters, and the following day Janet and Solita transported her to the American Hospital in Neuilly suffering from appendicitis. Their *chambres* became an editorial room when Margaret Anderson, Jane Heap, and Georgette Leblanc moved in to assemble the final number of the *Little Review*. In the confusion they spilled green ink on the sheets, provoking the patrons' wrath, and perhaps inspiring Margaret's choice of a going-away present—a complete repainting of Janet's fireplace. Hemingway often ascended to the fifth floor, too, and always occupied the same yellow chair; and one night F. Scott Fitzgerald slept outside in the hallway, tight.

"The only directive Harold Ross ever gave me for writing the 'Letter from Paris' for his *New Yorker* magazine in the early summer of 1925 was . . . perfect. 'I don't want to know what you think is going on in Paris. I want to know what the French think.' That's the way Janet recalled the assignment

Ross issued in 1925, the maiden year of the magazine that printed her reports, profiles, and letters for the next fifty years. Ross condensed Janet's first two letters into one and published it in October over the signature "Genêt." A little startled to find her letter signed with a nom de plume instead of her own name, she asked Ross which of the three "objectionable" Genêts she knew he had had in mind. He never replied, but Janet later learned that Ross probably didn't know any of the three and had merely tried to make the name seem like a Frenchification of Janet.

Janet's early letters to the *New Yorker* combined instruction and chattiness. They were useful guides for the traveller coming to Paris, but they were limited in their scope. Gradually, she expanded her purview to include politics, focusing on the emergence of fascism in Germany at the same time she recorded the struggles of socialism to survive in France. Politicians always fascinated her—Leon Blum, Marshal Pétain, and Charles de Gaulle, for example—the latter being the one whose ascendancy to power she recorded with astuteness and clarity in countless letters. Celebrated literary figures, mostly friends such as Colette, drew her interest, too. Among the entertainers she described and helped to make famous was Edith Piaf. After watching her last public performance, Janet wrote that the singer, "ravaged" and "ill," dressed in black, "her pallid little moon face set in its sad, nocturnal smile," tottered across the stage to a microphone, and released that "great remnant of her life"—her voice.

Although Janet conscientiously fulfilled Ross's assignment to report what the French thought was going on in their country, she never lost touch with her Left Bank friends, even after the *New Yorker* began providing her with comfortable quarters in Right Bank hotels like the Continental and the Ritz. Turning the pages of *Paris Was Yesterday,* I again see that this is true. In 1929, she reported that Nancy Cunard had set up her Hours Press and would begin publishing books by Richard Aldington, Norman Douglas, and Ezra Pound; in 1933, she prepared New Yorkers for a literary event, the appearance of her friend Gertrude Stein's controversial book under the "sly inscription" *The Autobiography of Alice B. Toklas;* in 1935, she announced that another friend, Sylvia Beach, her finances at a low point, would sell important manuscript holdings. To all those she had known and continued to know on the Left Bank of the Seine, she remained a faithful friend, a steady, understanding, tolerant confrere.

Long before photographers like Jill Krementz immortalized Janet Flanner's craggy features, a young woman in Paris asked her to pose in the party costume she had assembled for a ball. She did, and Berenice Abbott took one of the most unusual, and by now very familiar, portraits ever made of the *New Yorker*'s Genêt. Gazing directly at the camera, wearing Sir Bache Cunard's Ascot top hat with two eye-masks, a silver and a black one, wrapped around it, a mannish blouse, a dark jacket, and wide-striped trousers, a look of soulful placidity on her face, Janet taunts the viewer to discover the person who has obligingly unmasked herself.

Janet Flanner (left) with James Jones, Thornton Wilder, and Alice B. Toklas at the exhibition "American Writers in Paris," Paris, 1959 *(Photo from the collection of Morrill Cody).*

At the time, 1925, Berenice Abbott was only twenty-seven and had just begun her career as an independent photographer and, I might add, as a competitor to Man Ray from whom she had learned much and for whom she had labored long and hard. Berenice was accustomed to hard work, however. The youngest of six children born in Springfield, Ohio, to parents who divorced while she was still a young child, Berenice grew up learning that taking care of oneself meant arduous work, loneliness, and developing a resolute and independent life. She graduated from high school, despite the demands of shifting alone, studied sculpture at Ohio State University, and in 1918 left Ohio (a state she much despised by this time) for Greenwich Village. Three years later, after a brief and disappointing course in journalism at Columbia, she went to Paris. There she became a pupil of Emile Bourdelle and attended classes at the Grande Chaumière. In addition, when she could afford it, she enrolled at the Kunstschule in Berlin. But shuttling between Paris and Berlin, even if only occasionally, came to an end in 1923 when she ran out of money. How she supported herself after that, she recently told an interviewer, she preferred to keep a secret, but, she added, "I never became a whore."

The patrician Janet Flanner as Uncle Sam at a fancy dress ball, Paris, 1925. The top hat Nancy Cunard's father wore when attending the races at Ascot *(Photo courtesy of Berenice Abbott).*

It was at this point that she joined Man Ray. Working with him, sometimes as model but more often as apprentice, she found immensely satisfying. It even brought her a little notoriety. One of Man Ray's first portraits of Berenice hung for years in the popular nightclub, the Boeuf sur le Toit. It was in the darkroom, however, that she felt most at home. "I had this knack for printing," she told Meryle Secrest. "I could feel the space in the print. That print would come up and I could feel the roundness of it. I believe . . . I had an uncanny sense about developing prints." With Man Ray's encouragement, she began to take her own pictures, often during lunch breaks. At times she photographed the same people he did. Since she was using his materials and studio, they agreed that half of her fees should be paid to him. It seemed a fair

Portrait of Berenice Abbott by Man Ray, Paris, mid-1920s *(Photo courtesy of Juliet Man Ray).*

arrangement at the time. What seemed increasingly unfair, however, was the salary he paid her, whether, as has been reported, it was ten francs a day, or 300 francs a week. For so little money, he was simply demanding too much work, and when the split fees she gave him exceeded the salary he paid her, she decided to go her own way. That was in 1926.

That same year she found a studio in the rue du Bac and announced that she had left Man Ray and was in business for herself. From her friends Bob McAlmon and Peggy Guggenheim, she received loans. From Bryher she received her first camera. By herself, she quickly organized an exhibit at the gallery Sacre du Printemps. It was a success. Her black-and-white portraits of James Joyce, Djuna Barnes, and Sylvia Beach drew enthusiastic comments. They were something new. They defied traditional ideals and methods of photography and presented a sensitive impression of the subjects without any analysis or study of character. We saw that they conveyed a broad simplicity without any conscious attention to detail. She made no attempt to romanticize her subjects.

For the next four years Berenice prospered. She took portraits of Jean Cocteau, Marcel Duchamp, Edna St. Vincent Millay, Margaret Anderson, Max Ernst, Princess Eugène Murat, Marie Laurencin, Thelma Wood, Bob McAlmon, and many others not so well known. To those who pointed out that she had set herself up in competition with Man Ray, Berenice replied: "We became unwitting competitors, which was ridiculous because his work was so different from mine." Her observation is sound, as their portraits of James Joyce, Peggy Guggenheim, and George Antheil illustrate. Where Man Ray's portraits reflect a certain imposed image, Abbott's reveal her belief, perhaps traceable to Eugène Atget's example, that the subject must be allowed to create its own image. Man Ray's portrait of Peggy Guggenheim, for example, asserts a bohemian sensuality that is achieved partly by dressing her glamorously in a cloth-of-gold evening dress by Poiret and a magnificent headdress by Vera Stravinsky. Abbott's, by contrast, shows a rather frail, intelligent woman, holding a pet dog in a firm embrace; in her expression there is a suggestion of humorous sarcasm.

Why, having made a success in Paris, would Berenice return to America? In February 1929 she spent a month in New York City. She enjoyed herself, marveled at the changing city, and decided to make it her home while she worked on the project that would establish her as an outstanding photographer in her own country. The new subject would be a profile of New York. The project may have been inspired, but not influenced, by the indefatigable photographer of Paris, Eugène Atget, who during his career supplied over ten thousand images of Paris to artists searching for subject matter for paintings. Atget, an obscure, penniless old man when Berenice met him in Man Ray's studio, made an immediate and incisive impact on her. "There was a sudden flash of recognition," she later explained. It was "the shock of realism unadorned." Without delay Berenice began to buy as many of Atget's prints as she could afford. She invited him to her studio and photographed him, at his insistence but her disappointment, in his "best" coat. When she went to his flat a few days later to show him the pictures she had taken, she was startled to learn that he had died. After months of struggle, she succeeded in purchasing (with help from Julien Levy) Atget's entire collection, and soon afterward she began the painstaking task of preserving and printing "the most beautiful photographs ever made." Atget, Berenice had often said, was a dedicated man, a man with a mission. Perhaps it was that sense of mission she discovered in him that explains her own apostolicism on his behalf. For years, she tried to place Atget's collection with various museums, always unsuccessfully. Likewise, art magazines and galleries took little notice, even those in France. And then in 1968 this stubborn custodian finally found a home for her treasures. The Museum of Modern Art purchased the whole collection for eighty thousand dollars.

Berenice Abbott's comprehensive study of New York continued to the end of the decade, until 1939. She photographed the city from top to bottom ("I believe I started with the waterfront and worked northward."). She was drawn to disappearing things—floating oyster houses, for example—and to new buildings like Rockefeller Center. To her great relief, after several years of financing her project alone, the Federal Art Project of the Works Progress Administration agreed to sponsor it and put her on a salary of thirty-five dollars a week and provided her with an assistant and a driver. Her finished portrait captures a city marked by contrasts (the old and the new, the small and the large jostle side by side). In the combination of dramatic interactions, one sees and feels the looming technological advances that threaten but never completely overwhelm the human. The recorder of Paris would have approved of his admirer's inspired efforts to portray the dynamism of another great city.

Also from Ohio came my lifelong friend Florence Gilliam, who for over fifty years lived in the city she adored above all others. I believe it was just prior to the Second World War that Florence operated a small public relations firm with another American woman. Among their first and largest clients was the Hotel de Crillon on the Place de la Concorde, one of the most distinguished and expensive hostelries in Paris. After the liberation of France, when Paris was striving to regain its former luster and magnetism, Florence arranged to move into the Crillon, the better to observe its daily life. She explained she could be a more effective spokesman for the hotel if she were actually a functioning part of it. The management concurred, Florence settled in, and even when her public relations business dissolved a few years later, she remained at the Crillon as a nonpaying guest and unofficial hostess for mainly Anglo-American visitors. For most of her long sojourn there she lived in the same cluttered, book-lined room (*Chambre* 61), handy to a tiny elevator *(deux personnes)* that would deposit her on the ground floor near the ornate entrance hall and lobby and not very far from the bar. In the magnificent dining room she ate her meals, usually alone, but sometimes with friends and guests, and every evening, punctiliously, she appeared in the bar, where I often joined her, for her customary drink of bourbon. As the years passed, Florence became known to thousands of people as "the little old lady of the Hotel de Crillon." She was still residing there in 1979 when she died at the age of ninety-two.

Just before the war erupted in 1939, Florence and I had finished writing a book we had started two years before. We called it *The Art of Living in Paris*. It was intended for people who planned to reside in the city for at least a year and who needed help with the problems they would face during their stay, particularly if they hoped to live on a minimum budget. It contained much practical information as well as a complete gazetteer of the seldom publicized sights of Paris. We even included a listing of unusual courses offered by universities and specialized institutions. We were proud of our book and very disappointed when, after accepting it, the publisher in America (Viking) delayed publication because of the threat of war. Then, after the war, so much

Berenice Abbott, Rutgers University, 1978 *(Photo courtesy of Rutgers University).*

had changed in Paris that our book, had it been printed, would have been of only limited use. The manuscript now resides at the University of Wyoming library.

In 1941, having witnessed the fall of Paris and the Nazi occupation (Florence lived for eight months under German domination), she returned to the United States via Lisbon. Determined to devote herself to beleaguered France, Florence became executive director, in New York, of public relations for American Relief of France, and when the war ended and she was once again in Paris, she remained with this organization. There her major accomplishment was supervising the construction of a youth center at the University of Paris, in the rue du Faubourg St. Jacques, not far from the old Montparnasse quarter where she had lived in the twenties. I saw the building the day it was turned over to the university in the presence of the minister of education. For her service, Florence received the Legion of Honor, an aware she proudly added to the Palmes Academiques and Medaille de la Reconnaissance Française.

I suppose that, besides being back in America after twenty years, what Florence had seen happen in France in 1940 and 1941, and the position she

Florence Gilliam, author and journalist, in Paris, 1940 *(Photo courtesy of Jacques Baron)*.

subsequently assumed to aid the country she had recently fled contributed to her decision to write what she called a "tribute" to France. In her foreword to the book she titled simply *France,* she spoke of how the sudden separation from her adopted country had affected her:

> For twenty years Paris was my home. In the spring of 1941 I left it to return to the United States. As my boat came into the harbor of New York, I felt something like the snapping of a continuity. Life had always seemed a chain . . . or quicksilver perhaps, which defies sharp beginnings and endings. Never was there a point at which to stop and look back, or peer ahead. That day, time seemed for once to stand still. The feeling of finality, or of pause, was only relative, of course. While some things stopped, others began. Yet in New York I sat down and asked myself a lot of questions. Here are some of the answers I have found.*

*Florence Gilliam. *France*. (New York: E. P. Dutton & Co., 1945), Foreword.

Florence Gilliam, Paris, late 1950s *(Photo courtesy of Jacques Baron).*

Florence's questions can all be compressed into one large query: What does France mean to me—aesthetically, emotionally, and spiritually? Her investigations allowed her to reflect on the arts—ballet, theater, painting, and literature—and the country, its history, people, and traditions. The results, redolent of what Edith Wharton wrote of imperiled France in 1915, can likewise be put into a single statement: France, because of its "age-old acquaintance with life, the practiced lucidity, the inexorable will, and the indestructible spirit" of its people, is "the fate of our civilization."

The adoration she felt for Paris and her adopted country had been intensified by the conflict that threatened to destroy what had become a necessary component in her life. Although always a quintessential American, Florence was at the same time one of the most complete Francophiles I have ever known. She was the perfect example of what Glenway Wescott meant when he said about another American living in France, Kay Boyle, "she was more completely abroad than the rest of us." From the time she arrived in Paris in 1921 until the day she died, Florence absorbed French life and allowed it to absorb her.

Florence's route from Ohio to Paris nearly duplicated the one followed by

Florence Gilliam at the Marbeuf theater, center of avant-garde drama, Paris, late 1950s *(Photo courtesy of Jacques Baron).*

Berenice Abbott, the common stopover for both women being Greenwich Village. But unlike Berenice, Florence had graduated (Phi Beta Kappa) from Ohio State University and had taught for several years in a Columbus high school before she moved to New York. Already in the habit of passing the summers in the city, where her single passionate indulgence was the theater, she grasped the opportunity to move to New York permanently when in the summer of 1920 she was offered a job running a Village bookshop called Sonia's. It was in that bookshop shortly after she had assumed her new position that she met the man whom she would accompany to Paris the following year. His name was Arthur Moss. A native Villager (Moss had actually been born there), Arthur was an amazingly energetic organizer and

A few participants in the Quat-z-Arts Ball, yearly celebration for the art students of Paris, 1922 *(Photo from the collection of Morrill Cody).*

promoter of a variety of activities, a skillful *raconteur,* and the single staff member of an animated little magazine distributed in the Village called the *Quill.* A short man with extremely bright eyes (in Paris he would be nicknamed Arthur Mouse), and "a mischievous child-like grin and an all round gamin quality," Arthur easily rivaled other Village characters like Maxwell Bodenheim and Bobby Edwards as one of the most colorful figures around. He appointed Florence *Quill's* managing editor and assigned her to write book and theater reviews along with Alan Ross MacDougal, once secretary to Isadora Duncan. Among other contributors Florence soon met were Harry "The Tramp" Kemp, Witter Bynner, William Zorach, Jo Davidson, Pierre Loving, and Arthur's ex-wife, the costume designer Millia Davenport.

In Paris, Florence and Arthur moved into a small hotel in the rue Delambre, around the corner from the carrefour Vavin and the cafés Rotonde, Dôme, and Coupole, all of which they soon made their hangouts. I remember, though, that as they became more familiar with the ambience of each place and its clientele, they adopted as their two favorites the Closerie des Lilas, which had preserved a literary character, and the old Bal Bullier across the street, where they enjoyed some big costume balls that must have been as sartorially spectacular as the Quat-z-Arts Ball Florence attended attired in jeweled breastplates and a G-string beneath a transparent gold skirt. Arthur appeared in a brief tunic.

Within a few months of their arrival, Florence and Arthur took an apartment in the rue Campagne Première and launched a magazine they named *Gargoyle*. It was the first English-language review of the arts and letters to appear on the Continent after the war. The cartoonist Wyn Holcomb designed the first cover, mistakenly drawing a chimère instead of a gargouille. Florence and Arthur took care of the technical and production chores and divided the reviewing assignments equally between themselves—Arthur writing book reviews and a humorous column called "Entr'Acte," and Florence covering music, ballet, and theater. Their first art director was Hungarian painter Ladislas Medyes, who was a theatrical designer and later consultant to Helena Rubinstein. Medyes was followed by Julian Levi, whose friends contributed a subsidy to the magazine. Among the artists whose work Medyes and Levi procured for *Gargoyle* were Jacques Lipchitz, Henri Matisse, Ossip Zadkine, Man Ray, Wyndham Lewis, Jo Davidson, and Max Weber. From their large circle of English and American friends, Florence and Arthur drew the literary content of the magazine—poetry from Malcolm Cowley, Hart Crane, Edna St. Vincent Millay, and Laurence Vail; short fiction from Robert Coates and James Stephens; criticism from Matthew Josephson and Gorham Munson. Sinclair Lewis, Hilda Doolittle, Bryher, Stephen Vincent Benét, and Robert McAlmon appeared in *Gargoyle* too, and in one number the editors printed several scores by *Les Six* composers.

Somehow they kept *Gargoyle* going a year and a half, until December 1922, when, their funds gone, they sadly notified loyal subscribers and readers it would close. Although it had never paid its own way, not to mention making a

Janet Flanner, Berenice Abbott, and Kay Boyle at Rutgers University conference "Women, the Arts, and the 1920s in Paris and New York," 1978 *(Photo courtesy of Rutgers University)*.

Four celebrated women of the Twenties: Janet Flanner, Berenice Abbott, Kay Boyle, and Lillian Hellman. Rutgers University conference "Women, the Arts, and the 1920s in Paris and New York," 1978 *(Photo courtesy of Rutgers University).*

profit, they had until the last minute hoped to find some means to extend its life a while longer.

The disappearance of *Gargoyle* did not deny Florence and Arthur outlets for their work. Arthur wrote articles for the English-language newspapers then being published in Paris and a gossip column ("Across the River") for the *Paris Times* that rivaled Wambly Bald's lively column "La Vie de Bohème." Florence took a position as managing editor of Fairchild's international magazine *Paris* (I also worked for Fairchild's), served as correspondent for *Theatre Magazine* (New York), and was a regular contributor to *Theatre Arts*, *The Arts*, and *Art and Decoration*. In 1927, however, they again became the prime movers in a little magazine. Called the *Boulevardier*, it was the expensive creation of a "continental socialite" and member of the Vanderbilt family named Erskine Gwynne. Using the *New Yorker* as a model, Gwynne hoped his venture would appeal to the wealthy Anglo-American colony in Paris. Gwynne himself provided much of the lighter material, while Moss, in addition to producing a column called "The Left-Over Bank," assumed all the managerial responsibilities. Florence contributed a monthly theater column, Irving Schwerke wrote music reviews, and Alice Perkins, of Fairchild Publications, reported on fashion. The *Boulevardier* attracted a few American and English writers, among them Ernest Hemingway, Noel Coward, Michael Arlen, and Louis Bromfield. It also united a group of outstanding cartoonists, both French and American, who then, or later, gained a prominent place in contemporary

humorous or character studies. But the formula that was responsible for the
New Yorker's popularity in America did not work for Gwynne and the
Boulevardier in Paris. Gossipy stories, articles about horse racing, golf, and
yachting, and Gwynne's spicy and sometimes malicious column "Ritz Alley"
substantially outweighed the magazine's artistic offerings, and four years after
he started it Gwynne brought the *Boulevardier* to a close.

Janet, Berenice, and Florence, all permanent exiles from their native
American Midwest, drew from French culture the substance of their art and
from French life a point of view that shaped how they lived and formed what
they believed. They were astute observers with the talent to preserve what
their senses disclosed to them. They created in words and images a memorable documentation of a deep and pulsating manner of living at a time of
incessant artistic vitality in a place that gave stimulus and guidance to those
responsive to their interior yearnings. They took what Paris offered, freely and
unstintingly, and returned it abundantly in artistic tokens of grateful appreciation.

The Innkeepers

IN 1921 when I first became an habitué of Montparnasse the focal point for the artists and writers was a big sprawling café on the corner of the Boulevard Raspail called La Rotonde. In those days it was much bigger than it is today, and its inner sanctum was dark and mysterious. Men and women gathered around wooden tables to huddle over their drinks and whisper in low voices. Sometimes when you approached such a group the conversation would suddenly stop until you had moved out of earshot. They must be conspiring, you said to yourself, and doubtless they were if they were speaking one of the eastern European languages. Lenin and Trotsky are known to have frequented La Rotonde as did many others of foreign revolutionary purpose. La Rotonde also had a large terrace and in good weather the British and Americans, joined by their French friends, gathered to form a more open and hilarious contingent.

In those days a woman was considered vulgar if she smoked on the street and was even considered a little daring if she did it in a restaurant. So one fine spring morning when a good-looking American girl ordered her coffee and croissant on the terrace of the Rotonde and then calmly lit a cigarette, there was a craning of necks by the customers and consternation among the waiters. Her particular waiter rushed over to her table.

"Mademoiselle," he said in what he thought was a low and soothing voice, "it is not permitted for ladies to smoke on the terrace. If you will take a table inside I will bring your coffee and croissant."

"No," she said firmly, "I am going to smoke here."

"But mademoiselle, the rules . . ."

"Never mind the rules." The waiter retired to find the manager. A busy

Café du Dôme terrace, 1920s *(Photo from the collection of Morrill Cody).*

Café du Dôme terrace, 1920s *(Photo from the collection of Morrill Cody).*

little man came running. "Mademoiselle," he panted, "the rules do not permit it. You must go inside."

"I am staying here," she said even more firmly and in her best French. When he persisted in trying to move her inside, she got to her feet, gave him a disdainful look, and calmly walked across the street to the café opposite called Le Dôme. This café was much smaller than the Rotonde with a minute terrace and one main inside room largely filled with a billiard table. It was plainly a workman's café which served the typical *coup de rouge* as the main course for breakfast. She sat down on the terrace, and the waiter served her coffee and a croissant with no comment about her cigarette.

By late afternoon most of our group seemed to know about this incident and had decided that they would desert the Rotonde, forever. In a very short time the Dôme came to be known far and wide, certainly in Britain and America, as *the* place to go to see the notables of Montparnasse. The delighted owner enlarged the terrace and removed the billiard table. It was subsequently still further enlarged while the Rotonde finally went into bankruptcy. I do not know now the name of the young lady who caused this upheaval, but I think she did us all a service.

Later, Montparnasse was to have other distinguished cafés such as the Select and the Coupole, but they never attained the special character of the Dôme. One of its attractions was a waiter named Caesar, who had a great affection for his foreign clients. He was even known to give them credit, a rare procedure in café circles.

But at best the Dôme remained somewhat impersonal because of its size and rapid turnover. The Anglo-American groups, especially, felt the need of a smaller and more intimate gathering place and the first of these was the Dingo, just a few doors up the street behind the Dôme. It was owned by an American named Lew Wilson, but its greatest attraction was his wife, Jopie, a Dutch woman with a warm and gentle feeling for many of the Montparnassians. She opened up her arms and took each one to her ample bosom. They could tell her their troubles and be comforted. I think this was especially true for the women of Montparnasse who had no other "mother" to turn to when beset by the troubles of love or financial need or just someone to talk to. She did not neglect the men, but her special care was for the women. Among Jopie's special friends were Zelda Fitzgerald and Lady Duff Twysden.

The Dingo also had another asset in human warmth, namely its bartender, Jimmy Charters, who has been praised in print by many writers. Like Jopie, Jimmy was a sympathetic listener, a true friend, although he was always careful to keep his place, a rare combination. He was Irish and that helped a lot, but his unforgettable stock in trade was an infectious Liverpool grin. Jimmy had his own problems, however, and they were all related to alcohol. He would stay entirely sober for two or three weeks and then suddenly disappear for three or four days at a time, leaving the Dingo without anyone to serve behind the bar. Wilson finally fired him for these unexpected absences, but Jimmy immediately got another job in a nearby bar and took with him many of

The Select café as it appears today *(Photo from the collection of Hugh Ford).*

Interior of the Jockey Club, with decorations by artist-manager Hilaire Hiler, 1929 *(Photo from the collection of Morrill Cody).*

Dingo American Bar, with owner Lou Wilson and his Dutch wife, Jopie, about 1925 (Photo from the collection of Morrill Cody).

the Dingo's clients. Wherever Jimmy went most of the British-American groups would trail along after him, and especially the women who found him indispensable.

Jopie was not the only motherly type in Montparnasse. There was Madame Camille, who operated a hotel and bar on the rue de Tounon, and behind the bar there, too, was of course Jimmy. It was called the Trois et As (the trey and the ace), a somewhat bizarre name in either English or French. Jimmy told me that this was his "best" bar, by which I think he meant that it was the scene of more human drama than any other. Drama meant the beginning or the ending of a love affair, an occasional fight (though Jimmy, an ex-prize fighter, was quick to put down that sort of thing), sometimes political arguments which became overheated, and sometimes the antics of those who drank too much. But mostly it was love or its lack that made the world go round. On the quieter side there were those who sat and discussed their writing or their art or their adventures, but they created no drama. Through all this, Madame Camille sailed, laughed, put her arms around those who needed comfort, and remained calm and sympathetic.

But it is the story of Madame Pons which touched me most, and this is how it came about. Near St. Germain des Près is a little seventeenth-century street which runs between the busy rue de Rennes and the rue du Dragon. It is a narrow little alley, called rue Bernard-Palissy, without sidewalks and without notable buildings, but nevertheless with considerable old-world charm. To-day, it has taken on a certain cachet due to the presence of several attractive restaurants and shops, and a certain ugliness due to the presence of a large garage. But in the twenties its only noticeable landmark was a *maison numérotée*, so called because the street number was emblazoned on a lamp of colored glass over the door and by its sign inviting men with an hour to spare to visit the girls inside. Such establishments, completely legal in those days, were usually found in narrow little byways so that the customers were not likely to be noticed as they slipped in and out.

Farther up the street at number 14 was a modest student hotel, and it was there that I lived in 1921 and 1922, a most happy experience. This had come about through an accidental meeting with an American collegemate named Roy.

"Looking for a place to stay? Come along and meet Madame Pons. Perhaps she has a room free."

Madame Pons was a tall, thin woman in her late thirties, I suppose, and obviously a person of education and culture. Before the war she had been a trained nurse and had traveled in many countries, especially in the Middle East, but for reasons somehow connected with the war which I did not understand, she had given up her career to run this impoverished little hotel where, aided only by a scrubwoman, she did almost all the housework herself and from which she could hardly have derived much financial benefit.

Yes, Madame Pons had one free room, her best one, as it happened. It was one flight up, had two windows opening on the street, and was furnished simply but adequately with a comfortable bed, a large armoire, a chest of drawers, a table covered with a cloth of uncertain color, two chairs, and a wash basin mounted on a wooden stand. The place was spotlessly clean as was every room in the house. There was also a fireplace from which protruded a small potbellied stove. For around twenty dollars a month, I could have this room and breakfast, with laundry and mending included. I took it at once.

Life with Madame Pons began at seven in the morning when she shut our windows and built a fire in the little stove of each of her roomers, of whom there were nine, I believe. We had strict instructions to stay in bed until the room warmed up. At seven-thirty she returned with a large can of hot water, and a half hour later she appeared with a tray of coffee, toast, butter, and jam. If one of us took ill, Madame Pons, the registered nurse and unofficial doctor, was in charge. She saw to it that we were seldom ill.

The hotel was licensed to receive men only, and most of her customers were students at the Academie Julien round the corner on the rue du Dragon. When we came back in the afternoon around five o'clock, Madame Pons rebuilt the fire in each room, which would then last us until bedtime. The roomers were all young, of course, in their early twenties and of assorted nationalities. Roy and I and a chap named Roberts were Americans; there were two Frenchmen, three Argentines, and one Greek. The latter was one who did not attend Julien, but instead worked with the master Antoine Bourdelle and was said to be his star pupil. Through the Greek, Roy and I were allowed to visit Bourdelle from time to time, to admire his heroic sculpture, his stylized horses, and his statuesque nudes. He and his wife were most cordial to us, talking

A group of habitués at the Dingo bar, about 1925 *(Photo from the collection of Morrill Cody).*

about art and insisting that we have a glass of wine with the family. The studio is now the Bourdelle Museum near the Gare Montparnasse, and his daughter still lives there. At the hotel we were all friends and some of us generally gathered every afternoon either in Madame Pons's large ground floor room or in my relatively spacious place to talk about art and to drink tea gently spiked by Madame Pons with white wine and served in large glasses which burned the fingers. Occasionally, we would invite some of the American girls around St. Germain to join us, young ladies who were "doing Europe" with their parents or perhaps also studying in one of the art schools. Madame Pons liked the American girls in their starched cotton dresses because they looked so "wholesome," she said, and not like the French girls of the quarter. Cotton dresses, especially when starched, were unknown in France in those days, and because of that, one could distinguish the American girls blocks away. The "Americaines" sometimes brought their mothers with them, and for such an occasion Madame Pons inevitably changed her dress and brushed her hair.

One evening when we came back from the academy, however, Madame Pons was obviously upset by a summons she had received that morning from the nearby police station. "Madame Pons," the officer had said, "we know you, and we have nothing with which to reproach you, but a complaint about your hotel has been lodged, and we are bound to investigate. It is charged that you are running a house of prostitution without a license, and as you know this is a very serious matter. Your license permits you to rent rooms to men only. Do you, in fact, have any women living in your hotel?"

Madame Pons was indignant. She protested vigorously and demanded to know who had made this charge. The officer finally told her. It was the owner of the *maison numérotée* down the street. Her business was poor, and she was not going to permit competition from unlicensed Madame Pons.

"Monsieur le Commissaire," she assured him, "I am absolutely innocent. Come and see for yourself, talk to my roomers who are all poor students studying at the Academie Julien."

And so the next day, while all of us sat in our rooms drinking tea and trying to look as though we did not even know that girls existed, the officer arrived, made a cursory inspection of the building, and departed. But it did not end there. The madame of the *maison numérotée* renewed her complaint and this time stated that the prostitutes were girls imported from the United States. Madame Pons exploded. She told the commissaire that some lovely American young ladies had indeed come to the hotel to drink tea with her roomers but always in the presence of Madame Pons herself. These were very proper girls in starched dresses who even brought their mothers with them, *"riches touristes americaines."* What could be more proper? No bedroom door was ever closed. The inspector must come and see for himself. He said he would on the following Monday.

And so for several days we feverishly rounded up all our most starched American girls and a couple of their mothers, telling them, of course, that this would be a demonstration of American virtue which would astound the French. Monday they appeared, more of them than we had bargained for, and as a result we did not have enough glasses for the tea, though Madame Pons faced the situation by hurriedly buying a dozen new ones. There we were, all over the hotel, standing in the hallways or in the rooms with all the doors wide open, even those leading to rooms whose occupants happened to be absent. The inspector came, but when he took one look at all that giggling starch and the matronly stance of the mothers, he turned on his heels and departed. The complaint against Madame Pons was dropped for good.

It would be wrong to say that girls never spent the night at the hotel, though none of the very proper "Americaines" ever did. Madame Pons was a realist, and her nurse's training, she explained, had included teaching about the sexual problems of young men. Her roomers, she explained to each of us on arrival in the hotel, were permitted to bring a girl in for the night on Saturday once a fortnight. This was necessary and good for our health, she said. The girl must be clean and decent and, of course, not a prostitute. She favored one of the Julien models for the occasion, but did not insist on it. At holiday seasons such as Christmas and Easter, she tolerated a girl every week for a short time.

As you can see, Madame Pons had a deep motherly instinct which she poured out on her roomers, but she did not smother us with it, and it never made us feel cramped or encumbered. She wanted to do everything possible

Dingo bar, with Jimmy Charters and assistant barman, 1924 *(Photo from the collection of Morrill Cody)*.

Jimmy Charters with friends, including *Paris Tribune* reporter Leigh Hoffman (far right), 1928 *(Photo from the collection of Morrill Cody)*.

for us, but she never wanted to interfere in the slightest with what we ourselves wished to do. For the Americans, particularly, this at once made Paris a paradise of freedom. Madame Pons was never nervous and worrisome, and she always maintained a cheerful attitude despite what must have been back-breaking work to serve us all so well six days a week. Sundays we were on our own. She never complained, never talked about herself. She appeared to be alone in the world, for she received few visitors and no relatives. She seemed to live for us alone.

Then one day she asked Roy and myself to come down to her room for a glass of white wine. For once she was a little nervous, and we became edgy watching her. She refilled our glasses, and we waited anxiously.

"As you know," she began, looking down at the bed on which she sat and pulling at her sleeve with her hand, "I was fortunate enough to come from a fairly good family and to receive from them a thorough education including two years of medicine, training as a registered nurse, extensive reading in litera-ture and history, travel in many countries. Now I am running a small hotel without future. My only compensation in the last year or so has been my friendship with the boys who are my roomers and especially the two of you. Don't laugh at me. I am utterly serious."

"To me it seems wasteful that I cannot pass on to others some of the education and background I so laboriously obtained. I have therefore formed a plan which I would like to discuss with you. I want your reaction as young men who have the future ahead of you." She moved from the bed to a chair and this time looked at us directly, a golden light shining in her eyes. We murmured appreciative sounds, and she went on.

"My plan is simple: I must have a baby, a boy of course, to whom I can give all I know and help to find the things I do not know, a baby who will grow up to be a leader, a giant among men. Who knows, he might be prime minister or president." Tears welled up in her eyes. She wiped them away with a handker-chief, and continued to pour out all the great virtues that would seemingly be inherent in this genius—his kindness, his intelligence, his understanding, his farsightedness, but above all his keen and quick intelligence. Finally, she ran out of words, her mind in a far away dream, while Roy and I sat there not knowing what to say, slightly embarrassed by a show of emotion by a person so much older than ourselves.

"Of course," she said, pulling herself together with an effort to return to her usual practical manner, "I must have a father for this child and that is where I thought I would consult you. The father must be a man of recognized stature and education and great intelligence, a man who has arrived at an important position in life so that he, too, will have much to pass on to this child. And of course he must be a Frenchman. My child must be thoroughly French in all ways as befits a great leader among Frenchmen. Do you have any suggestions for a father?"

Roy and I were nonplussed, to say the least. We thought of the men around the quarter, of a distinguished artist like Bourdelle, and again we made murmuring noises of sympathy.

"I cannot go to national leaders like Poincaré or Herriot, because they might give a political coloring to my child. My child must be above party politics even though he will be a political leader of the French. I did think of one man, Doctor R——, whose office nurse I was in Cairo and with whom I worked later in Paris. He is a very distinguished surgeon, and I suppose you have heard of him. He has received many honors in many countries and is certainly considered a leader in his profession. What would you think of him?"

We hastened to agree that he would be excellent, but . . . but was she sure he would . . . accommodate her?

"That's the point. I don't know, but I can soon find out."

She stood up to show that her consultation with us was over. She swore us to secrecy, and we left with very mixed emotions. When we talked it over later, we decided that Madame Pons was a wonderful woman and that we would always try to help her if we could, but we had some reservations about the practicality of her plan. However, these French, they did remarkable things.

Next morning Madame Pons was as cheerful as ever, even more so as she delivered my breakfast.

"I telephoned the doctor last night and he remembered me at once. I am to see him this afternoon around six. I did not of course tell him what I wanted over the telephone. I want to explain everything in person, especially how I plan to devote my life to my son and bring him up to be a great Frenchman."

That afternoon she put on her best black dress with the pearls, the hat with the feather, and she had a certain gleam in her eye. If only the doctor also has a gleam in his eye, I thought.

By the time she returned, Roy and I had gone out to dinner, but when we got back around ten, she was still up and hailed us as we approached.

"Come in. I saw him. He agreed! I am so happy. He agreed, but of course there are some problems. Have some champagne. I bought it especially to celebrate, and it may be the last time I will be able to drink wine until my baby is born." Roberts happened along at this moment, and he was brought into the secret so that he too could have some champagne. "The problem is his wife. He will come here the first night she is away. My child, my child! He will be a wonderful child—and a great Frenchman."

Then the waiting began. Each morning with the breakfast, we asked about the doctor and she shook her head. Not yet, but soon. We began to wonder if he would ever arrive, but she seemed to have full confidence in the future father of her man of destiny. Then one day she received a *pneu*, and she hurried to tell us the news. He would be there tomorrow night and that was Christmas Eve. What a sign from the gods, what an omen!

By this time Madame Pons' other lodgers were in on the secret, and we were all aware of the doctor's arrival about ten that evening, for he came in a taxi, in itself a notable event in the rue Bernard Palissy in those days. We left the building quietly so that we would not disturb our guest—he seemed like "our" guest indeed—and went off to celebrate the occasion in the cafés of St. Germain. We all glowed with a certain inner satisfaction. Life was good. The future held promise. And tonight was Christmas Eve.

From then on Madame Pons was constantly exuding a radiance that affected us all, and soon we too were talking about this child as though he were already a leading light in the intellectual world of France. No one even suggested that "he" might turn out to be a "she" because that would be too humiliating. How could a woman be a great French leader? Madame Pons would not permit it. And then when she announced that her obstetrician had confirmed her pregnancy, we had another bottle of champagne with much laughter and singing and extravagant talk about the future of the child who, by this time, had been given the name of Roy. Madame Pons had decided that Roy was the most distinguished of her lodgers, and besides she thought the name Roy was a symbol because he would be a king among men—like Napoleon, perhaps, but better. De Gaulle, in those days had not been invented.

The days and weeks went by and Madame Pons maintained her exuberant spirit, dreaming of the day when unborn Roy would dominate the scene, when his writings and his spoken words would inspire Frenchmen to great deeds. Her eyes would look up to the sky and she would breathe deeply. "Ah, *mes amis*," she would say softly, as though to tell us how lucky we were to be there at the beginning. He would go to the Lycée Henri IV, she said, or perhaps Louis-le-Grand. Then after his *bac* he would study at the Sorbonne, law certainly, political science of course, literature, too, and art. Summers he would travel, Florence, Venice, Paestum, Salamanca, Heidelberg, Vienna, even New York and London. Then he would take a chair at the university, become the mayor of some small community near Paris, perhaps Fontainebleau. And then he must marry, of course, a woman with a little private income. If she had some nursing training, it would be useful, she thought.

But then one night I was wakened by a voice from the room below. It was Madame Pons calling to the concierge of the building across the street. That lady responded at once, and there was emotional conversation which I could not hear. The concierge left and a little while later a man arrived with a little black bag. More conversation, then quiet, and the doctor left. Next morning I asked the *femme de ménage* what had happened, but I already sensed the worst. Madame Pons had had a miscarriage.

For two days we did not see her, and when we did she looked somehow different, not only sad, but a little distant.

"Of course you will start again," we said and she replied that she would not. She had tried, but God must be opposed. She would not try again. Perhaps it had been a mistake in the first place. Yes, it must have been a mistake. She had been punished for presuming too much.

She took care of us as before, but more from duty than from warmth of feeling. Our closeness was gone and summer was coming and many of us were going away until the Académie Julien opened again in the autumn. I was returning to the United States, and when I came back a year later, Madame Pons had sold the hotel and moved to the suburbs, according to the concierge across the street. I took her address, but I did not write her. The joy of our association was gone. Today, if her son had lived, he would be in his fifties, a prime age for a great man to be preparing to take the leadership of his country's affairs.

L'Envoi

ERNEST Hemingway finished *A Moveable Feast*, his collection of sketches about life in Paris in the twenties, by saying that for him Paris had no ending, and that, like a wise and kind and generous friend, it returned whatever people brought to it.

The women and men I have written about in this book understood what Hemingway meant. No matter how brief or how long their stay in Paris, they never merely skimmed through. They came, they absorbed, they played, and they created.

All those I knew left behind their words, images, music—indeed, a portion of themselves.

Index

Abatino, Count ("Count Pepito"), 37–38, 40–41
Abbott, Berenice, 13, 161, 162–66, 170, 174
Académie Julien, 79, 180, 182, 187
Aiken, Conrad, 151
Aldington, Richard, 94, 95, 134, 161
American Conservatory (Fountainebleau), 55
Anderson, Lois, 152
Anderson, Margaret, 14, 30, 67, 149–58, 160, 165
Anderson, Sherwood, 27, 77, 135, 152
Anglo-American Press Association, 36, 51
Antheil, George, 54, 95, 135, 165
Aragon, Louis, 89, 93, 94, 95, 124
Arconada, Cesar, 96
Arlen, Michael, 92, 173
Arp, Hans, 71, 124
Art and Decoration (magazine), 173
Art of the Century (Guggenheim Gallery), 74
Arts, The (magazine), 173
Ashley, Lady Brett. *See* Twysden, Duff
Asquith, Margot (Lady Oxford), 91
Associated Negro Press, 96
Atget, Eugène, 13, 165
Auden, W. H., 96
Authors Take Sides on the Spanish Civil War (Cunard), 96
Autobiography of Alice B. Toklas, The (Stein), 80, 85, 103, 161

Baker, Josephine, 14, 33–44, 96
Bal Bullier, 171
Bald, Wambly, 173
Baltimore Sun, 24
Bankhead, Tallulah, 25
Barnes, Djuna, 11, 12, 71, 136–37, 160, 164

Barney, Alice, 132
Barney, Laura, 132
Barney, Natalie Clifford, 13, 15, 132–40
Baron, Jacques, 124
Beach, Cyprian, 20
Beach, Holly, 22
Beach, Sylvia, 14, 15, 19–32, 46, 78, 136, 158, 161, 164
Beaton, Cecil, 92
Bechet, Sidney, 33
Beckett, Samuel, 71, 95
Beecham, Sir Thomas, 91
Belle Epoque, 7, 20
Benét Stephen Vincent, 172
Bennett, Jo, 15
Bird, Bill, 19, 30, 31, 51, 94
Bird, France, 30
Blitzstein, Marc, 53
Blum, Leon, 161
Bodenheim, Maxwell, 151, 171
Boeuf sur le Toit (café), 163
Bouillon, Joe, 43–44
Boulanger, Lili, 54–55, 56
Boulanger, Nadia, 13, 53–56
Boulevardier (magazine), 173–74
Bourdelle, Antoine, 180–81, 185
Bourdelle, Emile, 162
Bowles, Paul, 53
Boyle, Kay, 12, 22, 70, 72, 169
Brancusi, Constantin, 71, 92
Braque, Georges, 71, 79
Breton, André, 89, 124, 125, 127
Bricktop, 14, 37, 40, 41
Broca, Henri, 121

Bromfield, Louis, 173
Brooks, Romaine, 13
Brown, Sterling, 95
Bryher. *See* Ellerman, Anne Winifred
Butts, Mary, 12
Bynner, Witter, 151, 171
Byrom, Lutrell, 100

Cadaques, 123, 125, 126, 127, 130
Calder, Alexander, 124
Campbell, Roy, 94
Cannell, Kitty, 15, 103, 104–05
Carroll, Dr. Robert, 65
Carter, Elliott, 53
Caruso, Dorothy, 158
Casino de Paris, 40, 41
Cézanne, Paul, 114
Chamson, André, 22, 27, 31
Chanler, Theodore, 53
Charters, Jimmy, 9, 62, 69, 84, 100, 101, 102, 177,
   179
Chevalier, Maurice, 41
Claudel, Paul, 22, 56
Closerie des Lilas (café), 79, 171
Coates, Robert, 172
Cocteau, Jean, 40, 71, 121, 124, 135, 165
Cody, Sherwin, 153–56
Cody, Mrs. Sherwin, 152–53, 156
Colette, 40, 135, 161
Copland, Aaron, 13, 53, 54, 55
Corbin, Alice, 150
Coupole (café), 171, 177
Coward, Noel, 173
Cowley, Malcolm, 172
Craig, Gordon, 143–44, 147
Crane, Hart, 172
Crosby, Caresse, 15
Crosby, Harry, 15
Crowder, Henry, 95
Crowley, Aleister, 25
Cubical City, The (Flanner), 159
Cunard, Lady (Maud Alice Burke), 91–92, 95
Cunard, Nancy, 11, 14, 89–97, 98, 100, 161
Cunard, Sir Bache, 91, 161

Dali, Anna Maria, 130
Dali, Elena ("Gala"), 125–31
Dali, Salvador, 124, 125, 126–31
Damrosch, Walter, 55, 145
Daniele (model), 110–12
Davenport, Millia, 171
Davidson, Jo, 171, 172
Dean, Harriet, 152, 153
de Casa Fuerte, Marquise Yvonne, 56
de Gaulle, Charles, 41, 161
de Gourmont, Remy, 133–34
Delmos, Jacques Chaban, 138, 140
Dell, Floyd, 151
Dingo bar, 9, 15, 60, 62, 100, 177
Dôme (café), 9, 79, 141, 171, 177

Doolittle, Hilda, 12, 172
Douglas, Norman, 94, 97, 161
Drummond, Sir Eric, 37
Duchamp, Marcel, 71, 121, 123, 124, 125, 129,
   130, 165
Duchamp, Tina, 125
Dudley, Catherine, 33
Duncan, Augustine, 143
Duncan, Elizabeth, 143
Duncan, Isadora, 13, 141–48, 160, 171
Duncan, Raymond, 75, 143, 148

Edwards, Bobby, 171
Eliot, T. S., 30, 153
Ellerman, Sir John, 25, 98
Ellerman, Anne Winifred (Bryher), 25, 27, 98, 164,
   172
Ellington, Duke, 40
Ellis, Havelock, 94
Eluard, Paul, 89, 124, 127, 156
Elwell, Herbert, 53
Erickson, Eric and Lee, 51
Ernst, Max, 69, 71, 74, 124, 125, 165
Esenin, Serge, 145–47
Ethiopia Betrayed—Imperialism. How Long?
   (Cunard), 96

Fairbairn, Sidney, 92
Finnegans Wake (Joyce), 28
Fitzgerald, F. Scott, 22, 57–60, 62–65, 77, 98,
   135, 160
Fitzgerald, Scottie, 65
Fitzgerald, Zelda, 14, 57–65, 98, 177
Flanner, Janet, 12, 22, 32, 34–35, 158, 159–61,
   174
Folies-Bergère, 35, 40
Ford, Ford Madox, 22, 103, 135, 153, 159
Ford, Hugh, 97
Foujita, Tsuguhara, 117
France, Anatole, 135
France (Gilliam), 168–69

Gabin, Jean, 41
Gargoyle (magazine), 172–73
Gervasi, Frank, 86
Gide, André, 22, 135
Gilliam, Florence, 31, 166–74
Graham, Sheilah, 64
Grand Man: Memories of Norman Douglas (Cunard),
   97
Graves, Robert, 94
Green Hat, The (Arlen), 92
Green Hills of Africa, The (Hemingway), 84
Gris, Juan, 82
Guevara, Alvaro, 91, 92, 94
Guggenheim, Florette, 66
Guggenheim, Peggy, 15, 66–74, 164, 165
Gurdjieff, Georges, 156
Guthrie, Pat, 100–01, 102, 103
Gwynne, Erskine, 173, 174

Hall, Adelaide, 14
Hall, Radclyffe, 136–38
Hamnett, Nina, 13
Happy Failure, The (Solano), 159
Harris, Frank, 25
Harris, Roy, 53
Harrison, Barbara, 14
Heap, Jane, 14, 153, 155, 157, 158, 160
Hecht, Ben, 152
Helion, Jean, 72
Hemingway, Ernest, 9, 11, 19, 22, 25, 28, 31, 45,
    57, 59–60, 75, 77, 79, 82, 84, 92, 100, 101–07,
    117, 121, 156, 160, 173, 188
Hemingway, Hadley, 15, 25, 45–52, 60, 101, 102,
    103, 105
Hemingway, John Hadley Nicanor, 47, 51
Hemingway, Pauline Pfeiffer, 49, 51, 84
Herrick, Myron T., 37
Herriot, Edouard, 27
Henderson, William Penhallow, 150
Henderson, Wyn, 71
Henry-Music (Crowder), 94
Hiler, Hilaire, 121
Hoffman, Hans, 74
Hogarth Press, 92
Holcomb, Wyn, 172
Holms, John, 71
Hotchner, A. E., 105
Hours Press (Cunard), 94–95, 97, 161
Hughes, Langston, 95, 96
Hugnet, Georges, 84
Huxley, Aldous, 92

Imbs, Bravig, 84
In Our Time (Hemingway), 51, 94

John, Augustus, 92
Jolas, Eugene, 14
Jolas, Maria, 14, 31
Josephson, Matthew, 172
Joyce, Giorgio, 24
Joyce, James, 11, 22, 23–25, 28, 77, 153, 155,
    164, 165
Joyce, Lucia, 24
Joyce, Nora, 24–25

Kemp, Harry, 171
Kandinsky, Wassily, 71
Kenyatta, Jomo, 95
Kiki (Alice Prin), 14, 117–22
King, Clinton, 107
Kisling, Moise, 117
Kokoschka, Oscar, 92

Ladies Almanack (Barnes), 137
La Maison des Amis des Livres (bookshop), 20, 22
Larbaud, Valéry, 22
"La Revue Nègre," 33, 34
Laurencin, Marie, 165
Lawrence, D. H., 25

Leblanc, Georgette, 155, 156, 158, 160
Léger, Fernard, 34
Le Navire d'Argent (magazine), 25
Lettres à l'Amazone (Remy de Gourmont), 134
Levi, Julian, 172
Levy, Harriet, 81
Levy, Julien, 68–69, 131, 165
Lewis, Sinclair, 172
Lewis, Wyndham, 92, 153, 172
Lindsay, Vachel, 149, 151
Lion, Jean, 41
Lipschitz, Jacques, 172
Little Review, 14, 23, 67, 151–58, 160
Loeb, Harold, 66, 100, 101–06
Loving, Pierre, 171
Lowell, Amy, 151
Lowenfels, Walter, 94
Loy, Mina, 12, 68, 69
Luhan, Mable Dodge, 76, 79, 82

McAlmon, Robert, 11, 22, 25, 27, 77, 98, 164,
    165, 172
McBride, Henry, 77
MacCown, Eugene, 92, 94
MacDougal, Alan Ross, 171
MacLeish, Archibald, 27
Madame Camille, 15, 179
Madame Pons, 15, 179–87
Maeterlinck, Maurice, 155
Making of Americans, The (Stein), 77
Mansfield, Katherine, 156
Martin, Flossie, 14
Masters, Edgar Lee, 149, 151
Matisse, Henri, 79, 82, 172
Mauriac, Claude, 138
Maurois, André, 27
Medyes, Ladislas, 172
Menuhen, Yehudi, 56
Mercer, Mabel, 14
Milhaud, Darius, 56, 135
Millay, Edna St. Vincent, 165, 172
Miller, Henry, 12
Mills, Florence, 14, 33
Miró, Juan, 124
Mistinguett, 41
Models, 108–10
Modigliani, Amedio, 114, 117
Moffat, Curtis, 92
Monnier, Adrienne, 14, 19, 20, 22, 25, 27, 46
Monroe, Harriet, 149, 151
Moody, William Vaughn, 151
Moore, George, 91, 94, 97
Moorhead, Ethel, 14
Morgan, Evan, 91
Moss, Arthur, 170–73
Motherwell, Robert, 74
Moveable Feast, A (Hemingway), 84, 103, 188
Mowrer, Paul Scott, 52
Munson, Gorham, 172
Murat, Princess Eugène, 15, 165

Murphy, Gerald, 58–59
Mytchetsky, Princess, 54, 56

Negro (Cunard), 95, 96
New Review, The (magazine), 14
New Yorker, 158, 159, 160, 161, 173, 174
Nichols, Robert, 92
Nightwood (Barnes), 71
Nin, Anaïs, 12

Outlaws (Cunard), 92
Out of this Century (Guggenheim), 70

Padmore, George, 95
Parallax (Cunard), 92
Paris, 8–17, 159
Paris (magazine), 173
Paris Journal (Flanner), 159
Paris Times (newspaper), 173
Paris Was Yesterday (Flanner), 159, 161
Pensées d'une Amazone (Barney), 132
Perkins, Alice, 173
Perkins, Maxwell, 62, 63
Petain, Marshal, 161
Pfeiffer, Gus, 49, 51
Piaf, Edith, 161
Picabia, Francis, 124
Picasso, Pablo, 71, 79, 80, 82, 125, 130
Piston, Walter, 53
Plain Editions (Stein–Toklas), 77
Poeter, Virginia, 125
Poetry, A Magazine of Verse, 149, 150, 151
Point Counter Point (Huxley), 92
Pollock, Jackson, 74
Portrait of the Artist as a Young Man, The (Joyce), 153
Poulenc, Francis, 56
Pound, Ezra, 13, 77, 79, 93, 94, 95, 132, 135, 153, 156, 158, 161
Putnam, Samuel, 121

Quat-z-Arts Ball, 171
Queneau, Raymond, 124
Quill (magazine), 171
Quinn, John, 155

Raval, Maurice, 56
Ray, Man, 92, 117, 120–22, 125, 129, 130, 162, 163, 164, 165, 172
Read, Herbert, 71
Reynolds, Mary, 71, 123–25, 129, 130, 131
Riding, Laura, 94
Rilke, Rainer Maria, 135
Romains, Jules, 22, 156
Rose, Sir Francis, 79
Ross, Harold, 160, 161
Rossi, Carmen, 116–17
Rothko, Mark, 74
Rotonde (café), 113, 171, 175, 177
Rubinstein, Helena, 121, 172

Rudge, Olga, 13

Sabana de Costa, Lidia, 127
Sandburg, Carl, 149, 151
Sarrasan-Levassor, Lydie, 125
Save Me the Waltz (Zelda Fitzgerald), 58, 62–63
Schmitt, Florent, 135
Schönberg, Arnold, 56
Schwerke, Irving, 173
Secrest, Meryle, 163
Sélect (café), 100, 177
Sevareid, Eric, 86
Shakespeare and Company (Beach), 30
Shakespeare and Company (bookshop), 19, 22, 25, 27, 28
Singer, Paris, 144, 147
Sitwell, Osbert, 91
Smith, Bill, 102, 103
Smith, Melville, 13, 53
Solano, Solita, 158, 159, 160
Sonia's (bookshop), 170
Soutine, Chaim, 117
"Spain" (Auden), 96
Spanish Civil War, 96
Speyer, Darthea, 31
Statue in a Field (Solano), 160
Stearns, Harold, 15, 103
Stein, Gertrude, 10, 11–12, 14, 22, 23, 53, 75–88, 103, 134, 135, 161
Stein, Leo, 79–81, 82
Stein, Michael, 81
Stein, Sara, 81
Stephens, James, 172
Stewart, Donald Ogden, 101, 102, 103
Stravinsky, Igor, 56
Stravinsky, Vera, 165
Sublunary (Cunard), 92
Sun Also Rises, The (Hemingway), 14, 92, 101, 102–06
Surrealism, 71, 123–25

Tabia, Rosalie, 15, 112–16
Tanguy, Yves, 71
Tanner, Allen, 84, 155
Tchelitchev, Pavel, 84
Teasdale, Sara, 151
Terry, Ellen, 143
Theater Arts (magazine), 173
Theatre Magazine, 173
These Were the Hours (Cunard), 97
This Quarter, 14
This Side of Paradise (Fitzgerald), 63
This Way Up (Solano), 159
Thomson, Virgil, 13, 53, 54, 55, 84
Three Lives (Stein), 77
Three Mountains press, 51
Tietjens, Eunice, 150, 151
Titus, Edward, 121
Toklas, Alice B., 22, 23, 31, 75, 77, 78, 79, 80–88
transition (magazine), 14

Tree, Iris, 91, 94
Trois et As Bar, 15, 179
Trotsky, Leon, 175
Twysden, Duff (Lady Brett Ashley), 14, 89, 92, 98–107, 177
Twysden, Sir Roger, 100, 101
Twysden, Tony, 100
Tzara, Tristan, 124

Ulysses (Joyce), 23–24, 25, 28, 67, 151, 153, 155
Uncertain Feast, The (Solano), 159
Utrillo, Maurice, 117

Vail, Apple, 72
Vail, Clotilde, 67, 69, 70
Vail, Clover, 72
Vail, Katie, 72
Vail, Laurence, 66–72, 172
Vail, Pegeen, 70, 71, 72
Vail, Sindbad, 70, 71, 72
Valéry, Paul, 22, 56, 135
Vechten, Carl Van, 77, 85
Ventadour, Fanny, 72
Ventadour, Jacqueline, 72
Vivien, Renée, 133

Walling, English, 19
Walsh, Ernest, 72
Walsh, Sharon, 72
Warner, Sylvia Townsend, 95
Weaver, Harriet, 23
Weber, Max, 172
Well of Loneliness, The (Hall), 136
Wescott, Glenway, 103, 169
Wharton, Edith, 169
Whistler, James McNeill, 114, 116, 117
Whoroscope (Beckett), 95
Wilder, Thornton, 27, 31, 77, 85, 88
Williams, William Carlos, 95
Wilson, Jopie, 15, 177, 179
Wilson, Lew, 177
Wood, Thelma, 165
Woolf, Leonard, 92, 93–94
Woolf, Virginia, 92, 93–94

Yeats, W. B., 153

Zadkine, Ossip, 172
Zito, 37
Zorach, William, 171